THE ROAD LESS TRAVELED

A Journey Through the Degrees of the Scottish Rite

Michael J. Sekera 32° K∴ C∴ C∴ H∴

ISBN: 978-1-7348652-0-2 (Amazon Print)
ISBN: 978-1-7348652-1-9 (IngramSpark) PAPERBACK
ISBN: 978-1-7348652-2-6 (IngramSpark) HARDCOVER
ISBN: 978-1-7348652-3-3 (Smashwords)

For bulk purchase and for booking, contact:
Universityoffreemasonry@gmail.com
Michael J. Sekera, 32°, KCCH

Because of the dynamic nature of the Internet, web addresses or links contained in this book may have been changed since publication and may no longer be valid. The content of this book and all expressed opinions are those of the author and do not reflect the publisher or the publishing team. The author is solely responsible for all content included herein.

Given the arcane and varied nature of some of the source material, content has been drawn from various sources within and without the Masonic fraternity. While effort has been given to cite sources where known and established, the author acknowledges that some sources are impossible to verify and apologizes in advance if proper credit was omitted in any way.

Artwork: Original oil paintings by Bro. Robert H. White, 32°, from the Hall of Scottish Rite Regalia at the House of the Temple in Washington, D.C. Used with permission of the Supreme Council, 33°, S.J., U.S.A.

Cover Art: "The Camp": original artwork courtesy of
The Craftsman's Apron and Brother Patrick Craddock.

100% of the book proceeds will be donated to the California Scottish Rite Foundation in support of its programs, including vitally needed speech, language, and literacy therapy to children in California.

RiteCare Childhood Language Centers of California
a program of the
CALIFORNIA SCOTTISH RITE FOUNDATION

Dedication

Masonic labor est pure a labore. Qui quaerit ad hauriendam Masonic merces in auro et argento, et confunderis. Stipendia a Mason sunt in commercio cum invicem; sympathia begets sympathia, misericordiam begets misericordiam, helpfulness begets helpfulness, et hi mercedem a Mason

(Masonic labor is purely a labor of love. He who seeks to draw Masonic wages in gold and silver will be disappointed. The wages of a Mason are in the dealings with one another; sympathy begets sympathy, kindness begets kindness, helpfulness begets helpfulness, and these are the wages of a Mason.)

—Benjamin Franklin

Acknowledgments

My thanks to Illustrious Robert Davis 33°, G∴C∴ for his encouragement to have this book published. There are many other Brothers out there without their help this would never have become a reality.

Thank you to Illustrious John R. Heisner 33°, PGM California for your constant education of the craft. Illustrious Ray Godeke 33° helped greatly with the process arranging everything. There are very many other people I would like to thank and I would surely forget a few. I must simply say a big thank you to all who have assisted me in this process - in particular to my wife Abeer and my children Emily, Alexandra and Michael. Who above all others have been my greatest supporters throughout the preparation of this work.

Honor those who have come to pass and recognize the impact they made upon your life. For in these moments, we will come to find it was a true privilege to be among them.

Contents

Preface

Freemasonry—one of the oldest fraternities—boasts approximately 5 million members throughout the world. Its objective has always been to enable members to erect lifetime foundations upon lessons of virtue and morality. Among the several concordant masonic bodies is the Ancient & Accepted Scottish Rite for the Southern Jurisdiction of the United States of America. Adding to the fraternity's rich spiritual ceremonies, the Scottish Rite teaches lessons about "equilibrium" through 32 separate masonic degrees. Since its inception in the mid-1700s, the Scottish Rite has attracted numerous authors, scholars, and writers who have published an extensive volume of masonic educational material.

Michael Sekera's extensive commentaries on the Scottish Rite degrees is a significant addition to Masonic literature. No individual Mason has ever been empowered to define Freemasonry or its meaning. That has been left up to the individual Mason in consultation with the Great Architect of the Universe. But Brother Sekera's commentaries give us a new voice, a different perspective to consider, and an opportunity to challenge our existing point of view.

Serving as Venerable Master of the Scottish Rite Valley of Palm Springs, California, Brother Sekera has been an active masonic scholar since his initiation into the fraternity in 2008. His interest in the fraternity and its leadership has pointed him out as one of today's Masonic leaders. His opinions have been formed throughout a decade of study and are worth understanding. Current insights into ancient teachings are extraordinarily valuable to the body of masonic education.

It is my earnest hope and expectation that California Masons, as well as Masons around the globe, take the time to expand their knowledge by reading Michael Sekera's commentaries.

John R. Heisner, 33°, PGM California

Introduction

Robert G. Davis, 33°, G∴C∴

We have enjoyed a kind of renaissance in Masonic writings over the last quarter century. Largely influenced by the academic world's rediscovery of Freemasonry's historical influence on men and civil society over the past three hundred years, coupled with a realization by Masonic authorities that the once heavily guarded hidden secrets of Masonic ritual are now readily accessible to anyone through the world wide web, and thus, aren't so secret after all; the world's oldest fraternity is receiving considerable new attention. There have been more books published about Freemasonry in the past three decades than were published in the century prior to our time.

Self-publishing software has also given a voice to many Masonic writers interested in things relating to the symbolism, esotericism, philosophy, ethical aims, and moral principles outlined in Masonic teachings. Some of this is good; some merely expressive. But all of it gives Freemasonry a public image for readers that has not before been in the public domain.

While much is now available to interested readers, there has been very little literature penned in America about the Scottish Rite of Freemasonry; a branch of Masonry that is widely considered to be the college course in Masonic instruction. Perhaps very little is needed, as the Scottish Rite is governed by national Bodies that have their own research departments overseen by professional staff members. These highly trained and qualified historians are now sharing much of the archival materials of the Rite's history that have long been preserved in files not available to the outside world. The scholarship being made available to the rank and file Scottish Rite Masons residing in geographic areas across the United States is now inspiring many brothers to make an individual study of the Rite.

This enthusiasm is beginning to take root as more books are being published by brothers who wish to share their own interpretations of the lessons presented in the 29 Degrees which are conferred in their own States and Valleys. This book is one such example of this new and growing interest in the Scottish Rite.

In the chapters presented in this work, Brother Michael Sekera has outlined what he believes to be the central themes and teachings of the Degrees governed by the four Bodies which make up the Scottish Rite. From the 4th to the 32nd Degrees, Sekera presents the essays he penned as a student of the College of the Consistory, administered by the Valley of Guthrie in the Orient of Oklahoma. This curriculum was created to encourage Scottish Rite men to write essays on the teachings of the Rite. The purpose of the College is to provide a venue for Scottish Rite Masons to further explore the basis and meaning of subjects presented in the ritual and lectures of the Rite. The essays and research papers are the means used by the students to express their conclusions and findings. These writings are preserved and serve as a reflection of the student's progress in development and understanding of the lessons of the Scottish Rite. And, in collection, these writings illustrate the breadth of considerations and conclusions arrived at by those individuals who make up the College's student body.

While we can expect to see other enthusiastic writers share what they have penned in their own self efforts, and we encourage them to do so, there is one element that will likely remain missing in all of these works. What was the composition of the ritual of the first three Degrees that was originally conferred by the Scottish Rite?

It is a daunting question, as the degrees of Entered Apprentice, Fellowcraft, and Master Mason (the first three degrees of Masonry) are known to have only rarely been conferred in America. The reason for this is that the first three degrees of the Masonic Order have been governed by Grand Lodges since their inception. The Scottish Rite degrees came to America after 1763, some 30 years after Masonry was first established by Grand Lodges organized in the Colonies. If the degree system promulgated by the Rite was to survive, it made good sense not to compete with the already established authorities over the first three degrees of Masonry. And this is precisely what happened with the development of the Rite's governing authority, established with the creation of the first Supreme Council of the Ancient and Accepted Scottish Rite in Charleston, SC. in 1801.

The degrees of the Scottish Rite came to the Western Hemisphere via a patent issued to Stephan Morin by the second Grand Lodge of France sometime between 1764 and 1791. Morin had been charged with compiling a system of

25 degrees in 1763, which was named the "Order of the Royal Secret." This collection of degrees was made up of seven classes, the first of which were the degrees of Entered Apprentice, Fellowcraft, and Master Mason. Morin was given the authority to appoint men to confer the Order in the Western Hemisphere. By 1791, this system of degrees was known to have been conferred in Jamaica, New Orleans, New York, as well as other cities along the Eastern Seaboard. The newly established Supreme Council added eight more degrees to the system, which made the Scottish Rite a body of Masonry governing 33 degrees. In a subsequent compact issued by the Supreme Council, the first class of degrees were set aside by that Body to assure that the first three degrees of Masonry would remain under the jurisdiction of the previously established authority of Grand Lodges. One of the original nine members of the Supreme Council, Alexander Francis August de Grasse-Tilly, who was made a Deputy Inspector General in Charleston in 1796 under the Order of the Royal Secret, later became the primary actor in spreading the newly created Scottish Rite throughout Europe and the Caribbean. He was made a Mason in a Parisian Lodge in 1783. It is known that members of this French Lodge also became members of a Lodge in Saint Dominque. It was this body of men, working under Morin's patent within the Grand Orient of France, who promulgated the Order of the Royal Secret that was adopted in Charleston.

The first class of these degrees were rituals that originated in the Masonic rituals of both the Ancient and Modern English Grand Lodges. Research that has recently been uncovered by Arturo de Hoyos, the Grand Archivist of the Supreme Council, and Josef Wages, who has done much research into the origin of craft degree rituals, has revealed that the rituals promulgated by the Order of the Royal Secret were essentially a modified French translation of a popular Masonic exposure *The Three Distinct Knocks.* Thus, the early degrees conferred in the Order of the Royal Secret were of English origin, translated into French in 1797. It is known that this ritual was worked by the Ancient York Masons of South Carolina. It was a derivation of the English work that became what we know today as the Pike rituals of the first three degrees, which are kept in the archives of the Supreme Council.

With this brief introduction of the origins of the first class of degrees known as the Order of the Royal Secret, we have a much clearer understanding of the complete origins of the degrees which became the Ancient and Accepted Scottish Rite.

What is left for those of us who take a serious interest in what the Scottish Rite offers in Masonic knowledge is to enjoy the interpretations made of the lessons of the Rite by those fine men who are willing to share with the Masonic world what they have learned through their own study and effort. Brother Sekera gives us in these pages his observations about the teachings of the Scottish Rite. As in everything Masonic, we are to learn what we can learn from our brothers, and, in so doing, add to our own stores of wisdom.

1

4th Degree
Secret Master

The 4th Degree (The Secret Master) is one of the Ineffable Degrees. These degrees compile the 4th through the 14th degree and are called Ineffable Degrees because of their principal purpose. The purpose of these degrees is to investigate and contemplate the ineffable name of Deity. The Duties of the 4th Degree – The Secret Master is to practice Silence, Obedience, and Fidelity. The important symbols of this degree are the color black with silver tears, Adoniram, the key of ivory, the blazing star, the wreath of laurel and olive leaves, the great Masonic camp, the three pillars, and the nine Masonic virtues. In association to these symbolic meanings is the Apron of the degree.

According to Rex R. Hutchens in *A Bridge to Light*, it is described to be "white and edged with black, and it has black ties. These two colors symbolize the grief suffered by the Masons upon hearing of the master Hiram's death and the loss of the word. In addition, they are illustrative of the dualist nature of the universe containing light and darkness, good and evil, truth and error." When we associate the 4th degree with light and darkness, good and evil, and truth and error, we are to always follow the three great pillars of wisdom, strength, and beauty. They are Truthfulness, Endurance, Independence, Justice, Mercy, Equity, Silence, Devotion, and Attainment. Furthermore, the flap is sky blue with an open eye embroidered upon it in gold.

According to *Morals and Dogma,* this denotation describes the sun as the "great archetype of light, the Ineffable Deity. In its center is a 'Z' embroidered in gold, and around it are two crossed wreaths of laurel and olive. The jewel is a small ivory key with a black 'Z' upon the wards. It is worn suspended from a broad yellow ribbon edged in deep blue or black." The gold symbolizes the light emerging from darkness. Also denoted are the initials C.a.M., which stands for Clavis and Mysterium, the "key to the mystery." According to *Morals and Dogma,* "The jewel of the Master is a small equilateral triangle of gold emblazoned with the Greek letter's iota, alpha, and omega at the apexes. On the reverse are the Samaritan characters **Yud**, **He**, and **Vau**; three letters, with **He** duplicated, are used to form the Ineffable Name of Deity, called the Tetragrammaton, usually pronounced as Yahweh. The significance of the letter 'Z' is esoteric and thus is not proper to be discussed here. This is the initial of the password of the 4th degree, and in the Hebrew numerology of the Kabbalah, its equivalent letter had the value of 7, a number familiar to all Masons." The ceremony strikes a familiar setting, but there is no plot because the purpose of this degree is not so much to illustrate virtues as it is to lay the foundation for the entire system of the Scottish Rite Degrees.

Duty and its importance in the Scottish Rite Masonry are stressed in the ceremony; the duties of the Scottish Rite Mason are not to be performed in the hope or expectation of earthly rewards or honors but in the simple expectation of personal satisfaction. These duties form the path, which leads to the object of the Masonic quest, the True Word. The wreaths of laurel and olive symbolize the hopeful expectation of success in that search. The square is a reminder that the candidate has begun a great journey; however, it is not a simple journey.

In the reception of the 4th degree – Secret Master, the senior deacon crowns the secret master with a garland of laurel and olive. Laurel is an emblem of victory and triumph and was thought to be sacred to Apollo, the Greek god of light. The olive is an emblem of fruition, in hopeful expectation of that person's ultimate success and final victory. Then, the Venerable Master invests that same person with a key of ivory, the jewel of this degree. The letters on the cordon signify Clavis and Mysterium. This comes with a hope of a true understanding of Freemasonry and the ability to use its principles to wisely regulate one's life and conduct. The letter Z upon the wards of the key is the initial letter of the traditional password of this Degree, which is … and signifies the … in the east. This Degree explains some symbolism, such as the columns of wisdom, the all-seeing eye (or Masonic eye, or Eye of the universe), which now represents the suns as the source of light without intending any offense to its more traditional interpretations, the letter "G", which symbolizes the representative of the true God, and the blazing star, which symbolizes the search for truth.

In history, the "Masonic Eye" has led to many questions toward many fraternal societies, including Freemasonry. It is a symbol showing an eye surrounded by rays of light or a glory that is usually enclosed by a triangle. It is interpreted as representing the eye of God keeping watch over humankind. The triangle within the circle symbolizes the Grand Architect of the Universe. The circle signifies the universe, and the three sides are wisdom, strength, and beauty; or more properly, wisdom, power, and harmony. The Tree of Life, which is supported by the familiar Masonic pillars of wisdom, strength, and beauty, is emblazoned with nine circles forming three triangles and a final circle at the base representing the material world. These circles are symbols of the attributes of God that may be seen as manifested in particular virtues. These nine virtues are the true and shining jewels of a Master; compared with these, silver, gold, and precious stones are as worthless as the common earth from which they came. Nonetheless, the traditions of Freemasonry contain many representations, symbols, and associations that consist of much more than just the Apron, the letter "Z", or The Eye of the Universe. In brief, the use of symbolism lies at the heart of our traditions, which ultimately follows Freemasonry's eclectic use of symbols to permit the presentation through a variety of teachings, cultures, faiths, and philosophies.

2

5th Degree
Perfect Master

First off, the legend of this degree consists of a yearly ritual that takes place as a symbolic representation of death and rebirth of a particular Master Mason to live as an imitation of a perfect master (to live a perfect life). This ceremony, practiced from 1883 to 1935, represents the death and re-enactment of the burial of Master Hiram Abif ordered by King Solomon. This funeral ceremony teaches the sobering lessons of death and requires the candidate to prepare a last will and testament while in the preparation room of this degree. This purpose is to impress upon the candidate the uncertainty of life.

To live a perfect life, i.e., to live as a Perfect Master, the Master Mason is expected to have a sense that life is short and to be contemptuous of life. The idea of living a "perfect" life is to be aware of death and prepare diligently for what will happen after life. The Master Mason must acknowledge that death may take him, as well as anyone else, at any moment and have a concept that life is fleeting. The major idea is to "set your house in order," which simply means that we do not have time to waste. In addition, we have a duty to our families and our loved ones to see that our affairs are in order and that those we love are well taken care of when we depart this life. Leaving our families unprepared and not taken care of is something we, as Masons, can not do.

The lessons of this degree include nobility, which, according to the 5th degree – Perfect Master, the noblest portion of humanity is virtue for virtue's sake. Living a virtuous life would include being scornful of life. In addition, being always ready to die for a great principal that goes beyond just oneself is a sense of commitment the Master Mason would be obligated to in order to live as a perfect master and thus live a "perfect" life. Living a perfect life, expecting and preparing for death, and commemorating funeral ceremonies for our G.M.H.A. are all attempts to regard death not as the worst end that can befall a man but a common reality that we all face. Living a "perfect" life also requires always being willing to engage in self-sacrifice in the case of duty or as honor shall require it. The most excellent rewards of human virtue are the approbation of good men. This is a reminder to the Master as well as all Masons to do that which is right simply because it is right. Having the ability to do what is right is gained through honesty and industry. If you master these skills, when you die (whenever that will be), others will see that you have accomplished as much as possible honestly, and you can feel that satisfaction for yourself.

In *Morals and Dogma*, Albert Pike expands on industry, saying that idleness is the burial of a living man. This means that an idle person is so useless to any purposes of God and man that he is like one who is dead, unconcerned with the changes and necessities of the world. He continues saying that an idle person lives to spend his time and eat the fruits of earth like vermin or a wolf, and when his time comes, he dies and perishes, and that person will not have lived a life of virtue and nobility as a Mason who lives a "perfect" life would. Furthermore, to learn and to do is the soul's work. Knowing that you're doing something through virtue is an example of living a life full of principle. The duties of every Mason who desires to imitate Master Hiram, who would be living a "perfect" life, is said by Pike to sleep little and to study much, to say little and to hear and think much, to learn that we may be able to do and then do earnestly and vigorously whatever may be required of us by duty and by the good of our fellows, country, and mankind.

Not only is industry required of all Masons, especially the Master Mason who is selected to be the Perfect Master, but honesty must be accomplished to live a perfect life. It is expected that the duty of a Mason as an honest man is plain and easy; it requires Masons to be honest in contract, sincere in affirming, simple in bargaining, and faithful in performing. The selected Master Mason is not to lie at all, neither in a little thing nor in a great, neither in substance nor in circumstances, neither in the word or deed. It is required that a Perfect Master must avoid that which deceives or is false. This would be expected from a Perfect Master who wants to live a perfect life. Furthermore, it should be the earnest desire of every Perfect Master to live and deal and act like no man on earth is poorer because he is richer. Finally, Pike says to be careful because you are not due because "thou receive no wages."

Being one of the selected Master Masons to represent Hiram in a symbolic death and rebirth ceremony and one who is expected to live a perfect life in imitation of Hiram Abif would classify him as being a man who leads a wise and virtuous life. We should always keep our houses in order for we know not when our journeys upon this earth shall end. We should ask for God's aid to live well so that we may die well. Imitating Hiram means to live the "perfect" life. This would mean being a Perfect Master whose heart never can grow old, whose eyes are bright when youth has fled, whose ears are never dull or cold, whose lips can speak, though speech is dead. Living a "perfect" life is the responsibility taken by the newly selected Master Mason, who lives in such a way as to set an example that originated by Master Hiram. This life consists of knowing about death, preparing for it diligently, making sure loved ones are well taken care of after death, knowing that death may take any of us at any moment, seeing that our affairs are in order, being contemptuous of life, not fearing death, being encouraged by the fact that life is fleeting, and making our lives full of virtue, nobility, honesty, industry, and order. This ultimately reminds us that we should live a life with the most excellent rewards and, ultimately, live a perfect life.

3

6th Degree
Confidential Secretary

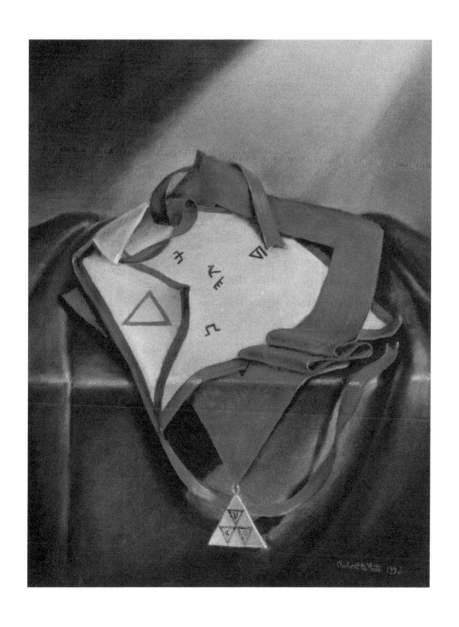

I t is the duty of the Mason to think better for the benefit of his neighbor. This means that the duty of the Mason is to be quiet instead of aggravating difficulties as well as bringing together those who are severed or estranged. Further duties include keeping friends from becoming foes and to persuade foes to become friends. This can only be made possible by a Mason controlling his own passions, not being rash and hasty, not being swift to take offence easily, and finally, not being angered easily. Being a peacemaker in everyday life is the duty of a Mason. Furthermore, it is the duty of a Mason to control their own temper and govern their own passions without getting out of line. You must keep peace and harmony among all men and especially the brethren. Last but not least, a Mason must remember, above all, that Masonry is the realm of peace. A Mason should remember that there must be no dissension but only that noble emulation that can best work and best agree.

Being a peacemaker not only consists of following morally correct ideals like benevolence, disinterestedness, and acting as a peacemaker but also consists of fidelity and zeal in the performance of everyday duty for every Mason. In addressing the virtues presented in this degree, Pike does not discuss them in the lecture; rather, he discusses the importance of duty, inferring that the Mason should be faithful to duty and perform his duty with zeal. In addition, benevolence, disinterestedness, and acting the peacemaker are explained in terms of generosity. Duty is in the moral magnetism that controls and guides the true Mason's course over the tumultuous seas of life. And to perform that duty, the performance is the Mason's sole care whether the performance is rewarded or not. It doesn't matter that this performance is watched by any witnesses and what he does will forever be unknown to all mankind. Being generous should be a personal benefit, and it shouldn't matter to anyone other than oneself.

According to benevolence, we should either be more severe to ourselves or less so to others and consider that no matter what good anyone can think or say of us, we can tell him of many unworthy and foolish and perhaps worse actions of ours, any one of which, done by another, would be enough, for us, to destroy his reputation. Generosity comes from benevolence because Masons must be kind and affectionate to one another. There is a major need to be much more of the spirit of the ancient fellowship among us. When it comes to each other's faults, Masons should express so much tenderness, forgiveness, solicitude for each other's improvement, and good fortune (somewhat of a brotherly feeling) that it shouldn't be a shame to use the word "brother." Benevolence also includes listening to others being praised without making an objection or making disparaging comments. A Mason has to learn to think the advancement of thy brother is not a lessening of thy brother.

Lacking disinterestedness and generosity is enough to exclude a man from the society of the Masons. He should show these qualities both in acts and in his opinions of men and his constructions of their conduct. Generosity and a liberal spirit should be in every Mason. This is to make men to be humane, genial, open-hearted, frank, and sincere. It should be in every Mason to earnestly do good, be easy and content, and be well-wishers of mankind. If a man wants to be a Mason or a gentleman, he needs to be generous, liberal, and disinterested. It is important to be liberal, but only of that which is our own; to be generous, but only when we have first been just; to give when we deprive us of a luxury or a comfort—this is Masonry indeed.

We should always strive to fulfill the role of the peacemaker. Often, disagreements are the result of simple misunderstandings that can be easily cleared up most of the time but which grow and fester into major confrontations if not resolved. As Masons, we all have a duty and obligation to others, both inside and outside the fraternity, to make life better and less contentious. We have an absolute obligation to care about others and to work for their interests. This is where generosity can benefit not only Masons but mankind, and this can be accomplished by the 6th degree.

In *A Bridge to Light*, Hutchens asks who can sum up the horrors and woes accumulated in a single war: "Masonry is not dazzled with all its pomp and circumstance, all its glitter and glory. War comes with its bloody hand into our very dwellings; it takes from ten thousand homes those who lived there in peace and comfort, held by the tender ties of family and kin. It drags them away to die untended of fever or exposure in infectious climes; rise no more, to be borne away in awful agony to noisome and horrid hospitals. The groans of the battlefield are echoed in sighs of bereavement from thousands of desolated hearths. There is a skeleton in every house, a vacant chair at every table. Treasures are expended, those which would suffice to build ten thousand churches, hospitals, and universities or rib and tie together a continent with rails of iron. If that treasure were sunk at sea, it would be calamity enough, but it is put to worse use for it's expended on cutting into veins and arteries of human life until the earth is deluged with a sea of blood. This is why every Mason should take fidelity, zeal, disinterestedness, benevolence, and acting the peacemaker into their lives; the benefits can be great to oneself as well as humanity that will provide every Mason with the duties needed to always be rewarded."

4

7th Degree
Provost and Judge

According to Webster's dictionary, retribution is "requital according to merits or deserts, especially for evil" but can also mean something given or inflicted in such requital. Inaction simply means idleness or the absence of action. The confrontation in this degree between retribution and inaction should be solved by justice, but it isn't as easy as many think it would be. Having the rights and privileges to bestow justice is a huge responsibility. At times, justice is the synthesis and compromise between retribution and inaction, depending on the scenario. Those people who are entrusted to administer the law must do so without any personal consideration. Having a personal vendetta would make judgment as a source to find justice unfair for those being judged. To be trusted with the position of provost, the judge cannot have a biased judgment for the bribes of the rich or the needs of the poor.

According to *The Scottish Rite Ritual Monitor and Guide*, the balance of being unbiased is the cardinal rule that no one will dispute, though many fail to observe it. To give a person a fair chance to resolve a problem, a judge would have to find the balance between retribution and inaction. This may lead to a synthesis and compromise between the two, depending on the situation. To do that, the person in power of bestowing power must divest themselves of prejudice and preconception, as well as wait patiently, remember accurately, and weigh carefully the facts and the arguments offered. They also must not leap hastily to conclusions or form opinions before they have heard the story. This is an obstacle that judges have to endure to ensure fairness as well as pure justice. Furthermore, a judge must not assign to the act either the best or the worst motives but those they would think it just and fair for the world to assign to it if they themselves had done it.

Human-administered justice can be on a hit-or-miss basis. Human emotions can readily be controlled to a certain extent. Once a human emotion is strong within a person and they have a personal vendetta in their lives, that may cause a very unfair judgment of someone else who commits certain crimes. Once something wrong is done, it cannot be undone, and it produces its own consequences. The wrong that is done contains its own penalty. Human-administered justice can sometimes be hasty, for if a person does not follow *The Scottish Rite Ritual Monitor and Guide* rules and guidelines for provost and judge, then it would be unfair to hold these standards to the person being judged. It is also said in *Morals and Dogma* "that it is not an arbitrary and vindictive act, but an ordinary and logical consequence and therefore must be borne by the wrongdoer, and through him may flow on to others. It is the right of every mason to avoid the commission of any injustice and acts of wrong and outrage."

We know little of the real merits or demerits of any fellow creature; therefore, it is not within the realm of any Mason's (or any human being's) responsibility to make any judgments before considering the full situation. These simple solutions that should be fairly easy to avoid can just as easily cause an uproar when it comes to the nature of human-administered justice. In *Morals and Dogma*, the concept of justice is explored from three principal points of view: consequence attends our every action, we should be just in judging other men's motives, and we can only be just when charitable. It concludes that Masonry does not seek to take the place of religion, but like religion, acknowledges a higher law than that of man. If a person is having a hard time with injustice, or any wrongdoing for that matter, they should follow the following instructions from the heavy burden of provost and judge: The judge must himself be impartial, cautious, merciful, and of pure morals. Only a false judge pardons errors in himself and not others. A judge must be aware of the grave responsibility he bears. A judge must inform himself fully of the law he is called upon to enforce. An unjust judge will be smitten by God. Remorse will pursue the corrupt judge beyond the grave. Judge not unless you are willing to stand under the same judgment. Understanding these guidelines led me to believe that many other people would see human-administered justice to be a form of mistrial, as it can be unfair.

It is very hard to explain human emotions. The basis of the argument of rejecting human-administered justice circumnavigates around the idea of human emotions and their effects on a judge who is meant to administer justice. If a human who is bestowed with this responsibility does follow the morally correct guidelines, then people would never need to worry about any wrong judgment or any wrongdoing by a person in an official position who is meant to seek justice. With the world we live in, this may not always be the case, and although it's unfair for many (whether the judge or the person being judged), it's how this world is maintained on an even keel. Nevertheless, when it comes to retribution and inaction, it is within the hands of these officials who are trusted to use their power for the common good of man, not for their own personal benefit in order to impart justice. In conclusion, let the true Mason never forget the solemn injunction necessary to be obeyed at almost every moment of a busy life: "Judge not, lest you yourself be judged; for whatsoever judgment you give to others, the same shall in turn be given to you." This lesson is taught to the Provost and Judge.

5

8th Degree
Intendant of the Building

There are various symbolic meanings of this degree, as stated by Rex R. Hutchens: "The aprons are white, lined with red and with a green border. The center is an embroidered nine-pointed star, and over that a balance. There is a triangle on the flap with Phoenician letters at each angle. The three colors white, red, and green, which are the chief symbolic colors of Scottish Rite Masonry. These are to teach us to imitate the purity of morals and zeal for the service of Masonry which have made our deceased Master immortal in the recollection of men. The hangings of the lodge are lit by 27 candles which are arranged in three groups of nine, each forming a triple triangle. These are in front of the east, west, and south. Furthermore, in front of the Master, to the right, is a small table which lights five other candles, four forming a square with one taller in the center. Over the Master is a blazing star with nine points, in the center of which are the letters IHV, in either the Samaritan or Hebrew alphabet."

There is also the jewel, which is a delta of gold. On one side is engraved or enameled the Samaritan words "Ben-Khurim" in Samaritan or Hebrew, both meaning "nobles" or "freedom." On the reverse is the word "ached," meaning, "our only God, chief and source of all." The triangular shape plays a vital role because it is the most fundamental symbol of the Deity. Finally, the cordon is a broad watered crimson ribbon, worn from right to left with the jewel suspended from it by a green ribbon.

All of the previous symbols play a vital role in the various symbolic meanings and significance of the number nine (and its multiples). These key symbols tell every Mason to be benevolent and charitable with a demand that we correct our own faults and those of others, thus knowing that what a man knows goes with him and, therefore, transmit one's knowledge as well as labor, which is honorable if done with sobriety, temperance, punctuality and industry.

The number 27 was peculiarly significant to the ancient Pythagoras, as were all multiples of nine. The multiples of nine are unique in that their products are numbers composed of individual numbers which sum to nine; for example, 9 x 2 =18 and 1 + 8 = 9; 9 x 3 = 27 and 2 + 7 = 9. This process may be continued through 9 x 9 = 81 and 8 + 1 = 9. The number 9 was deemed significant since it was a cube of three, the Pythagorean number of Deity.

The important lessons of this degree include the teachings of benevolence and charity as emphasized by Pike. Every Mason is to be taught charity and benevolence, to be a brother who sets an example of such virtues, and to correct one's own faults as well as to endeavor to correct those of your brethren. The practice of charity and beneficence is to be practiced by all men, for, according to *Morals and Dogma,* "there will always be in this world wrong to forgive, suffering to alleviate, sorrow asking for sympathy, necessities and destitution to relieve." Nonetheless, the young men who were selected to take it upon themselves to finish the temple play a vital role in this degree's significance. Gareb the Hebrew, Zelec of Gebal, Satolkin the chief of the carpenters, Yehu-Aber the Phoenician, and Adoniram the superintendent of the work are symbols portrayed by the five candles lit during ritual. These five candles are meant to show every Mason that, like the five men selected, they must not only be charitable and benevolent, but they should sympathize with the working man, relieve his necessities, and view himself as the almoner of God's bounty, recognizing all men as his brothers. The Province of Masonry is to teach the truth that all men should aspire to be an enlightened citizenry and have an independent judiciary and economic order based on capital and labor.

In addition, this degree's purpose is to show every mason that the performance of work, whatever it is and no matter how important, is rewarding if done diligently. Dignity and importance are attached to work and those who perform it. We are taught the rights of the laboring classes and one's duties toward them. Every laboring man is your brother, entitled to your regard and assistance. When it comes to dealing with those who you work with, we need to remember to always practice the rules of benevolence and charity. We also need to remember to never deal harshly with those we employ or those we work with. We should never make false, unjust, or unreasonable claims against a person, for that would be unworthy and degrading. Every Mason should always aid a brother and his family, recognizing all mankind as our brothers. Capital and labor must not be adversarial but complementary and respectful, for this would only work if we cooperate to produce harmony.

In closing, the symbolism and the significance of this degree are portrayed through our rituals, and it is something every Mason should abide by in everyday life. These are not meant to change a man, but this is merely a way of life that not only every Mason but every man should follow. The key symbols show the charity and benevolence of the five very just, now-celebrated men who played a vital role in building the temple. Pike reminds us in *Morals and Dogma* that "these degrees are not for those who will refuse to explore the mines of wisdom in the teachings of the Scottish Rite. We may become more adept at uncovering and interpreting the meaning of the ceremonies and symbols of Masonry, but this is not sufficient. Only when we have learned to practice all the virtues they inculcate are we prepared to receive its lofty philosophical instruct and to scale the heights upon whose summit Light and Truth sit enthroned." Finally, I would like to conclude with a quote that I believe sums up the key symbols and significance in this degree: Knowledge without its application is of little or no value.

6

9th Degree
Elu of the Nine

The nature of the 9th degree – Elu of the Nine teaches all Masons the differences and similarities of education and enlightenment. These two concepts are very important in everyday life. These duties include to enlighten the souls and minds of every Mason, to instruct and enlighten the people, and to be vigilant to the interests and honor of our country. This degree's duties are among the most important in the craft: education, enlightenment, and patriotism. In *A Bridge to Light* by Rex R. Hutchens, the author explains that education and enlightenment are not simply schooling and the worldly understanding that derives from it; these duties weaken us to far higher and nobler aspirations. He further describes that we must learn to guard against all forms of tyranny, whether from the pulpit or the podium. We must enlighten our souls as well as our minds to do the work of Him that guides us, ministering to our own self-improvement and the welfare of our nation.

In classical politics, a tyrant is one who has taken power by their own means as opposed to hereditary or constitutional power. This mode of rule is referred to as tyranny. The word derives from the Latin tyrannous, meaning "illegitimate ruler," which, in turn, was derived from the Greek words meaning "sovereign master," although the latter was not pejorative and applicable to both good and bad leaders alike. In modern usage, the word "tyrant" carries connotations of a harsh and cruel ruler who places his or her own interests or the interests of a small oligarchy over the best interests of the general population, which the tyrant governs or controls. Many individual rulers or government officials are accused of tyranny, with the label almost always a matter of controversy.

The understanding of tyranny is important in this degree because it has a lot to do with every Mason's understanding of education and enlightenment. In Pike's lecture with a recitation of those qualities that aid and support patriotism, he sums up the duties of this degree: "In the simple mandate, protect and oppress against the oppressor; and devote yourself to the honor and interests of your Country." He also notes the contrast of earthly sentiments and worldly deeds and gives notice to the students of Masonry that here may be found the practical active virtue that distinguishes honorable men. And by the means of education and enlightenment comes the mission of Masonry, which is not to cause unrest in civil government but rather to support the statutes and administrators of lawful authority against the clamor of indecisive and tumultuous rebellion. Political power is a contract with the governed, and an abuse of that power breaks the contract so the parties are no longer bound to it. Therefore,

Masonry's teachings are a precarious balance between rightful, even if severe, government and the need to speak out against abusive misgovernment.

When it comes to enlightenment, most men have sentiments but not principles. The former are temporary sensations; the latter are permanent and controlling impressions of goodness and virtue (which were discussed in previous degrees). The former are general and involuntary and do not rise to the character of virtue. Everyone feels them. They flash up spontaneously in every heart. The latter are rules of action that shape and control our conduct, and it is these that Masonry insists upon. When this degree talks about enlightenment, it simply doesn't mean the action of being enlightened but also learning through education. Furthermore, Masonry is action and not inertness. It requires its initiates to WORK actively and earnestly for the benefit of their brethren, their country, and mankind. It is the patron of the oppressed, and it is the comforter and consoler of the unfortunate and wretched. It is the advocate of the common people in those things that concern the best interest of mankind. It hates insolent power and impudent usurpation. It pities the poor, the sorrowing, the disconsolate; it endeavors to raise and improve the ignorant, the sunken, and the degraded.

More or less, in *A Bridge to Light*, the author explains that what we have devoted ourselves to in this degree is defending weakness against strength, the friendless against the great, and the oppressed against the oppressor as well as being ever-vigilant and watchful of the interests and honor of our country. May the great architect of the universe give us that strength and wisdom that shall enable us to perform these high duties well and faithfully.

The lesson this degree is meant to teach every Mason is that ignorance is the principal enemy of human freedom. A free press is indispensable to true liberty. Remorse and guilt are God's punishment and more severe than that of man. Ambition creates tyranny and despotism.

When it comes to education and enlightenment for every Mason, their purity has been preserved by the cardinal tenets of the old primitive faith that underlie the foundation of all religions. Masonry is the universal morality that is suitable to the inhabitants of every clime, to the man of every creed. It has taught no doctrines except those truths that tend directly to the well-being of man. The use of education and enlightenment is the natural work of Masonry, and in this practical life, the use of all faculties in their proper spheres, and for their natural function. Love of truth, justice, and generosity, as attributes of God, must appear in a life marked by these qualities. This is the meaning of this degree's use of the term "enlightenment." After this degree, Masons learn the virtues that they should all follow. Nonetheless, the natural form of Masonry is goodness, morality, and living a true, just, affectionate, and self-faithful life. This is the motive of a good man, but above all, it is loyal obedience to God's law.

In education, Masonry does require and expect every man to do something within and according to his means, and there is no Mason who cannot do something, if not alone, then by combination and association. If Masonry stays true to its mission and Masons to their promises and obligations, there will be aid to what were once Masonry's great schemes for human improvement, not fitfully and spasmodically, but regularly and incessantly, then we may be sure that the results wanted will be attained and a great work done. And then, it will most surely be seen that Masonry is not effete or impotent, nor degenerated nor dropping to a fatal decay.

A Mason has an obligation to instruct and enlighten the people, replacing ignorance with knowledge. A main functional task of the fraternity is the growing want of people so that they are more and more fitted for the knowledge that Masonry offers, which also stresses the following virtues that not only are important for this degree but are important for the obligation that every Mason must possess. These include disinterestedness (altruism, the lack of selfishness), courtesy, devotedness, firmness, frankness, generosity, self-denial, heroism, and patriotism. Now, when it comes to education and enlightenment, men are prone to ignorance and error, and the reformer is almost always martyred. Because freedom and liberty are important to the Mason, he must strive to make them possible in the world. Freedom is not possible in a context of ignorance, so the Mason strives to replace ignorance with knowledge. This is what we support in scholarship programs and why we urge quality in education and insist upon good public schools that are supported by the community at large. This is also why individual Masons volunteer for adult literacy programs, support public and educational television, give to colleges and universities, and ensure that the information is freely available to all people.

So, education means more than just one person learning; it's important to educate others as well. It is in every Mason's duties to pass on the lessons and virtues to all of mankind. This truly is a means of protecting our nation, and a Mason's nation is important to him. We have to educate ourselves and have to be willing to be educated by things such as knowing that patriotism is a virtue and not an old-fashioned sentiment of which one should be ashamed. Furthermore, jubelum is the symbol of ignorance, and the sword of justice and the bloody head are symbols of the fit punishment for those who try to keep others in ignorance, in order that they might be more easily controlled or subjugated. This is the meaning of enlightenment. It further concludes that every Mason should take the lessons and virtues from this degree (as well as all degrees) and apply them to everyday life. With education comes enlightenment, but this doesn't mean that enlightenment only comes from education. It also comes from application. And though education may come from being enlightened, it also comes in many other different forms.

In closing, I would like to add a quote by Pike: "A man may be a good sort of man in general and yet a very bad man in particular; good in the lodge and bad in the world; good in public and bad in his family; good at home and bad on a journey or in a strange city. Many men earnestly desire to be a good Mason. He says so, and is sincere…" I believe that with education and enlightenment, not only the sentiment of it but the application and the truthful following of these virtues, a man can become exactly what Pike speaks about: a good Mason.

7

10th Degree
Elu of the Fifteen

In *Morals and Dogma*, Chapter X (Illustrious Elect of the Fifteen) "is devoted to the same ideas as those of the Elu of Nine. It also features some ideas that concern the cause of tolerations and liberality against fanaticism and persecution, politics, and religion. It also discusses educational instruction and enlightenment against error, barbarism, and ignorance. Pike explains that these objects you have irrevocably and forever devoted our hands, our hearts, and our intellect and whenever we are in the presence of this chapter of this degree, we will be most solemnly reminded of our vows taken at the altar." I would explain this very similarly to the way that Pike does: "The Brahmin, the Jew, the Mahometans, the Catholic, the Protestant, each professing his peculiar religion, sanctioned by the laws, by time, and by climate must need to retain it, and they cannot have two religions. Furthermore, the social and sacred laws adapted to the usages, manners, and prejudices of particular countries are the work of that man. All that ever existed has had a basis of truth. And all have overlaid that truth with errors. The primitive truth taught by the redeemer was soon corrupted."

I would go into further detail by also claiming that "Masonry is the universal morality which is suitable to the inhabitants of every clime to the man of every creed. It has taught no doctrines except those truths that tend directly to the well-being of man, and those who have attempted to direct it toward useless vengeance, political ends, and jesuitism have merely perverted it to purposes foreign to its pure spirit and real nature," just as Pike remarks. Pike also describes how easy it is for human indolence to linger near help and refuse to pass on further outgrows of religion.

As Pike remarked, "Masonry teaches, and has preserved in their purity, the cardinal tenets of the old primitive faith, which underlie and are the foundation of all religions... Masonry is the universal morality which is suitable to the inhabitants of every clime, to the man of every creed." This follows the 10th degree, and further, I utterly and completely believe this, even well before I began my journey in Masonry. This is best put by Pike's direct words, for they are very powerful. He states that "the latter is the true Mason, and the best and indeed the only good Mason is the person with the power of business who does the work of life. The upright mechanic, merchant, or farmer—the man with the power or thought of justice or of love—his whole life is one great act of performance of Masonic duty. The natural use of the strength of a strong man or the wisdom of a wise one is to do the work of a strong man or a wise one. The natural work of Masonry in practical life is the use of all the faculties in their proper spheres and for their natural function of Love of Truth, justice, and generosity as attributes of God must appear in a life marked by these qualities that is the only effectual ordinance of Masonry. A profession of one's convictions joining the Order assuming the obligations assisting at the ceremonies are of the same value in science as in Masonry. The natural form of Masonry is goodness, morality, living a true, just, affectionate, self-faithful life from the motive of a good man. It is loyal obedience to God's law."

I believe that Masonry is, exactly as remarked, not a religious belief. And because I believe in this strongly, I also believe that Masonry does teach us a lot. It teaches us that the good Mason does the things that are good, which comes through in our way of life. And these acts should be done with a love of duty and not merely because it is stated as law. Instead, these acts should be enacted by both man and God, but mainly, it should be commanded by that person's will to do it. Every Mason should be true to his mind, his conscience, his heart, and his soul, and he should feel little temptation to do to others what he would not wish to have them do to him. Furthermore, for the sake of his brother near at hand, he will deny himself. Masons' desire attracts in the line of their duties, both being conjunction. You find such men in all Christian sects, Protestant and Catholic, in all the great religious parties of the civilized world, including Buddhists, Muslims, and Jews. They are kind fathers, generous citizens, unimpeachable in their business, and beautiful in their daily lives. You see their Masonry in their work and in their play. It appears in all the forms of their activity; individual, domestic, social, ecclesiastical, or political. True Masonry within must be morality; without it must become eminent morality, which is philanthropy.

In addition, when talking about the cardinal tenets of the old primitive faith that are the foundations of all religions, I want to simply explain that according to *Morals and Dogma, the old theologies and the philosophies of religions of ancient times will not suffice us now. The duties of life are to be done; we are to do them consciously obedient to the law of God, not atheistically loving only our selfish gain. There are sins of trade to be corrected. Everywhere morality and philanthropy are needed. There are errors to be done away with, and in their place, we should supply new truths radiant with the glories of Heaven. There are great wrongs and evils in church and state and in domestic social and public life to be righted and outgrown. Masonry cannot in our age forsake the broad way of life. She must journey on in the open street, appear in the crowded square, and teach men by her deeds, her fife more eloquent than any lips.*

As Pike explains, a person who takes Masonry as religious belief falsifies and denaturalizes it. In this world, we will always come across other people who are very different from us, physically, personally, mentally, and religiously. I believe that what is the truth to me may not be the truth to another person. The difference is in men at their birth. No man is entitled to assert that he is right and claim that another man, who may be equally as smart, well-informed, and holding the opposite opinion is wrong. Each thinks that it is impossible for the other to be sincere, and each, as to that, is equally in error. Many beliefs of former and present times seem incomprehensible; they startle us with new glimpses into the human soul, that mysterious thing that makes us all unique. All we may do, as Masons, is what we have learned, and that is to teach others as we've been taught.

I truly believe that Masonry is in fact the universal morality that is suitable for all persons. Although many people in this world, due to multiple reasons, have their own separate beliefs and their own sets of morals that aren't based around Masonry, and even though I believe that Masonry would fit the life-styles of all different types of human beings in this world, it doesn't mean that any other person is a lost cause. Through the words of Pike and his remarks on the 10th degree, I can see that Masonry would best fit anyone, never depending on race, color, location, or any other prejudices. Explaining this chapter has been very hard to do, and although I may not grasp the concept as well as Pike has explained it, I've been an avid listener and follower as Masonry has taught me. I would further explain that because every man has the same right to hold his own opinion and faith, which may be similar or very different from ours, every person is within the grasp of the truth.

In closing, I would explain that in this degree, the Elu of the Fifteen, with liberty comes truth, and although we may ask ourselves what truth is, everyone should feel that it is quite possible that another person, who may or may not be as honest and sincere with himself, may be in possession of the truth. If Masonry will be true to her mission and Masons to their promises and obligations (if reentering vigorously upon a career of beneficence), she and they will pursue truth earnestly and unfalteringly, remembering that our contributions to the cause of charity and education deserve the greatest credit when it costs us something. If we will give aid to what were once Masonry's great schemes for human improvement, not fitfully and spasmodically but regularly and incessantly as the vapors rise and the springs run and as the sun rises and the stars come up into the heavens, then we may be sure that great results will be attained and a great work done. Then, it will most surely be seen that Masonry is not effete or impotent nor degenerated nor dropping to a fatal decay.

8

11th Degree
Elu of the Twelve or Prince Ameth

When we speak of "Masonic Education", we are needlessly redundant. Freemasonry is education and simultaneously moral instruction, spiritual enlightenment, and intellectual growth so that a man may come to know—and improve–himself. But this isn't supposed to be a solitary activity; Freemasonry is also a brotherhood. Masonry has taught me to believe that "He who will not endeavor to add to the common stock of knowledge may be deemed a drone in the hive of nature, a useless member of society, and unworthy of the care and protection of Masons." Together, the brethren seek "that which was lost." What was lost? Truth through enlightenment. It is that search after Truth that makes Freemasonry philosophical. Where there is a love of wisdom, education is the act of courtship, life is a school, and Masonry is work. It is believed, as said in *A Bridge to Light,* that to be free is the same thing as to be pious, to be wise, to be temperate and just, to be frugal and abstinent, and to be magnanimous and brave, and to be the opposite of all these is the same as to be a slave.

Unfortunately, every age presents its own special problems, most difficult and often impossible to solve. This is how, in a populous and wealthy country blessed with free institutions and a constitutional government, the great masses of the manual labor class are enabled to have steady work at fair wages, to be kept from starvation and their children from vice and debauchery, and to be furnished with that degree, not of mere reading and writing, but of knowledge, that shall fit them intelligently do the duties and exercise the privileges of free-men; even to be entrusted with the dangerous right of suffrage. We've dubbed education "the unspeakable Masonic word" because it seems like no one ever talks about it. So, at first, you're pretty much on your own. Life is a school. The world is neither prison nor penitentiary, nor a place of ease. Life is given for moral and spiritual training, and the entire course of the great school of life is an education for virtue, happiness, and a future existence. The periods of life are its terms: all human conditions are its forms; all human employments are its lessons. Families are the primary departments of this moral education; the various circles of society, its advanced stages; kingdoms and republics, its universities.

The belief that calls for education makes the assertion that every man has the potential to learn. According to *Morals and Dogma,* even the poor man is at school. He has to take care of what he learns rather than complain. He has to hold his integrity, his candor, and his kindness of his heart. He has to beware of his envy, his bondage, and his self-respect. Furthermore, he has to beware of the mind's drudgery and degradation. While he betters his condition if he can, he has to be more anxious to better his soul.

He must be willing even more; he can learn a lot from poverty, for it offers great lessons of fortitude, cheerfulness, contentment, and implicit confidence in God's Providence. *A Bridge to Light* also says: "...the school of life is carefully adjusted, in all its arrangements and tasks, to man's powers and passions. There is no extravagance in its teachings, nor is anything done for the sake of present effect. While the course of human life is a conflict with difficulties, and if rightly conducted, a progress in improvement. It is never too late for man to Learn."

When discussing the differences and similarities between education and enlightenment, we often find ourselves asking how one can lead to another and vice versa. We also ask ourselves how one may trigger, spark, or solve the other's problem. Education and enlightenment are well discussed by Pike in the form of the intelligent person. This person should always be informed of their rights, and they will soon come to know the power they possess. This process provides education. According to Pike, this cannot long be oppressed, but it is said that once all this has been done, a pyramid of needs and successes will form, with the top of the pyramid being society at a wretched compensation for the want of the solidity at the base. This is what is seen as education to a small part that plays a vital role.

Enlightenment provides sentiments, which are what most men have. But not all men have principles. The former are temporary sensations, the latter permanent and controlling impressions of the good. The former is something that can be seen to spark enlightenment, hence the difference between education and enlightenment. Therefore, the former are general and involuntary and do not rise to the character of virtue. Everyone, including every Mason, feels them. They flash up spontaneously in every heart; these are rules of action that shape and control our conduct, and it is these that Masonry insists upon.

This degree's duties are among the most important of the craft: education, enlightenment, and as implied by the 9th and 10th degrees, patriotism. Education and enlightenment are not simply schooling and the worldly understanding that is derived therefrom; these duties hearken us to far higher and nobler aspirations. We must learn to guard against all forms of tyranny, whether from the pulpit or the podium. We must enlighten our souls as well as our minds to do the work of Him that guides us, ministering to our own self-improvement and the welfare of our nation. As Pike remarked: "Masonry teaches, and has preserved in their purity, the cardinal tenets of the old primitive faith, which underlie and are the foundation of all religions... Masonry is the universal morality which is suitable to the inhabitants of every clime, to the man of every creed." This follows the 11th degree, and further, I utterly and completely believe this, even well before I began my journey in Masonry. This is best put by Pike's direct words, for they are very powerful. He states that the latter is the true Mason and that the best and indeed the only good Mason is the person with the power of business who does the work of life. The upright mechanic, merchant, or farmer, the man with the power of thought of justice or of love, he whose whole life is one great act of performance of Masonic duty. The natural use of the strength of a strong man or the wisdom of a wise one is to do the work of a strong man or a wise one. The natural work of Masonry is practical life, the use of all the faculties in their proper spheres and for their natural function. Love of Truth, justice, and generosity are attributes of God and must appear in a life marked by these qualities. That is the only effectual ordinance of Masonry: a profession of one's convictions joining the Order, assuming the obligations, and assisting at the ceremonies are of the same value in science, as in Masonry the natural form of Masonry is goodness, morality, living a true, just, affectionate, self-faithful life from the motive of a good man. It is loyal obedience to God's law. Education and enlightenment play a vital role in the self and improving one's self. Although education and enlightenment are described in the 9th, 10th, and 11th degrees, their importance is implied, taught, and explained in other degrees as well as other readings and stories. It is within every Mason to possess the power of education and enlightenment, for it teaches us how to live the noble life.

This is important for my next point: In the Elu of the Twelve or Prince Ameth, the apron is white-lined and edged and fringed with black, and the flap is black. In the middle is an embroidered flaming heart. According to *Morals and Dogma,* the cordon is a broad black watered ribbon worn from right to left. Over the flaming heart on the cordon are the painted or embroidered the words "Vincere Aut Mori," literally meaning "Death Rather than Dishonor." I truly believe that Masonry is in fact the universal morality that is suitable for all persons. Although many people in this world, due to multiple reasons, have their own separate beliefs and their own sets of morals that aren't based around Masonry, and though I believe that Masonry would fit the lifestyle of all different types of human beings in this world, not believing in Masonry doesn't mean that a person is a lost cause.

Through the words of Pike and his remarks on the 10th degree, I can see that Masonry would best fit anyone, never depending on race, color, location, or any other prejudices. Explaining this chapter has been very hard to do, and I may not grasp the concept as well as Pike has explained it. But as Masonry has taught me, I've been an avid listener and follower. I would further explain that because every man has the same right to hold his own opinion and faith and this may be similar or very different to ours, every person is within the grasp of the truth. The flaming heart upon the apron and cord are symbols of that zeal and devotedness that ought to animate all Masons and those noble and heroic souls that have in all ages suffered and sacrificed themselves for their fellows or their country. The motto is a solemn pledge that one would rather die than betray the cause of the people or be overcome through his own fault. The jewel is a sword of gold, suspended from the cordon and represents truth. The Elu of the Twelve has been given the title of the Prince Ameth and is also known as the Prince of Truth, for "truth is sharper than any two-edged sword."

As you have already noticed from my discussion of the 11th degree, in each degree, Pike clearly provides hints of future lessons and reminders of the past lessons. Often, he attributes a special meaning to a specific symbol or character mentioned in a degree. Here, we are informed that the previous Elu Degrees (9th and 10th) symbolize an independent legislature and indispensable feature of free government. The nine Elus represent the upper house; they are fewer in number, more mature in wisdom, and elected for longer terms than those of the lower house, symbolized by the Elu of the Fifteen. This degree should remind us of another institution necessary for true liberty: the trial by jury of the twelve men whose unanimous verdict is necessary to convict someone of a crime.

In closing, I should explain in this degree, the Elu of the Twelve or Prince Ameth, that with liberty comes truth, and although we may ask ourselves what truth is, everyone should feel that it is quite possible that another person, who may or may not be as honest and sincere with himself, may be in possession of the truth. According to *Morals and Dogma,* With Education and Enlightenment in mind; "if Masonry will but be true to her mission and Masons to their promises and obligations; if re-entering vigorously upon a career of beneficence, she and they will but pursue it earnestly and unfalteringly remembering that our contributions to the cause of charity and education. Then deserve the greatest credit when it costs us something the curtailing of a comfort" or the relinquishment of a luxury to make them, "if we will but give aid to what were once Masonry's great schemes for human improvement not fitfully and spasmodically but regularly and incessantly, as the vapors rise and the springs run, and as the sun rises and the stars come up into the heavens, then we may be sure that great results will be attained and a great work done, and then it will most surely be seen that Masonry is not effete or impotent nor degenerated nor drooping to a fatal decay."

9

12th Degree
Master Architect

Before I explore the symbolic significance and implications of the Star of David, also known as the Mogan or Seal of Solomon, I must first present background info about the 12th degree. In Masonic Degrees, candidates make a series of ceremonial prescribed circuits of the altar. This practice is known as circumambulation. It is derived from the ancient Romans, Semites, Hindus, and others. It is thought to have been a rite of purification. The sun was believed to travel around the earth. In the symbolic lodge, the circuits of the craftsmen at the installation of the officers symbolize the possession of the lodge by the new Master. In Scottish Rite Masonry, this ancient symbol of purification is adapted to represent a renewal of virtue through the performance of duty. This degree is filled with a number of symbols that carry teachings further past actual ceremonies.

Within the ceremony, the crimson flames on the hangings represent the zeal and fervency required in the pursuit of wisdom from which a new man arises, becoming renewed in virtue. The idea is symbolized in other degrees by the color green (which I will speak more about later). The flames should remind us of our earthly instruction of the Scottish Rite and will now help me, as well as all Masons, and lead us into the realm of morality to that of true philosophy. The lodge is lit by three great lights, one each in the east, west, and south. They are symbolic of the power, wisdom, and beneficence of the Deity, which were represented on the apron of the 5th degree by three concentric circles. Behind the Master in the east are the columns representing the five orders of architecture. We are told these columns should remind us that Masonry, like architecture, is and has been the same in all countries and in all ages. They are also representative of the five divisions of the Scottish Rite Masonry: Tuscan (the three symbolic lodge degrees), Doric (the fourth through fourteenth degrees), Ionic (fifteenth through sixteenth degrees), Corinthian (the seventeenth through eighteenth degrees), and Composite (the Chivalric and Philosophical degrees, the nineteenth through thirty-second).

In ancient times, the night skies played an important role in Masonry. Therefore, the North Star, also known as Ursa Major (the big dipper), and Venus, the morning star, are other important symbols incorporated in this degree. Ursa Major appears in the north of the lodge and is representative of the deity and faith. Venus is an emblem of the ever-approaching dawn of perfection and Masonic Light. It is here that we first encounter the Seal of Solomon: two interlaced triangles, one white and the other black. This symbol hints at the principle of duality and the parallel comparison between the two. In the center of the nine triangles, in old Samaritan characters, is one of the names of

God, a substitute to the Hebrew for the true name of God, which is ineffable. Hence, the second of the five divisions of the Scottish Rite Masonry are Doric, which represents the ineffable degrees (the forth through the fourteen).

Furthermore, this also shows how in depth this degree touches on symbolism. In order to become a Master Architect, any candidate assumes the character of Adoniram, who, according to Masonic tradition, was the first person to whom this degree was conferred. After the Master Hiram's death, five intendants of the building were appointed to assume the Master's duties. Adoniram, having gained superior knowledge and skill, was subsequently appointed Chief Architect of the Temple and the successor to the Master Hiram. The advancement of the Adoniram to Master Architect teaches us that the ablest, wisest, and best of every nation should be its leaders. This is a virtue we, today, may take for granted. It is something that I believe all Masons as well as all humans in this world can depend on. Because this degree and its legends did not occur in the time of Solomon, Masonry began early in the 17th century. The legends of the degrees are all symbolic and allegorical. We are urged strongly to learn them to understand the true allegorical meaning of this degree, in particular what the Master Hiram symbolizes. This explanation is not given in the ceremony, but there is a hint as to what his name means. The explanation that follows has various meanings, and is located at p. 81 in *Morals and Dogma*.

Nevertheless, according to the *Encyclopedia of Freemasonry*: "The interlacing triangles or deltas symbolize the union of the two principles or forces, the active and passive, male and female, pervading the universe... The two triangles, one white and the other black, interlacing, typify the mingling of apparent opposites in nature, darkness and light, error and truth, ignorance and wisdom, evil and good, throughout human life."

According to the Israeli Ministry of Foreign Affairs of King Solomon's Seal, I've summed up the literal, cultural, Masonic and today's Universal meanings to understand that "the legend of King Solomon's Seal, of the wondrous signet ring, which he received from heaven, is common to Judaism, to Christianity and to Islam. King Solomon's Seal, whose base is on the ground and whose tip reaches heaven, symbolizes a harmony of opposites, whose significance is manifold as much as it is multicultural. It reflects the cosmic order, the skies, the movement of the stars in their spheres, and the perpetual flow between heaven and earth, between the elements of air and fire. The Seal, therefore, symbolizes super-human wisdom and rule by divine grace. Through geometry, in which the Pythagoreans and their followers saw cosmic symbolism, the hexagram and the pentagram became an expression of heaven and its reflection on earth, the divine and its reflection in creation and of the connection between heaven and earth, between the macrocosm and the microcosm, and between spirit and matter. King Solomon's Seal combines strength and beauty, symbolism and illustrative quality and all within a geometric figure, the most important characteristic of Islamic art. The Moslem artist's love of geometry allows the true essence of King Solomon's Seal as a symbol of the connection between the two worlds to be expressed; in this context, it symbolizes the link between science, beauty and metaphysics, with elements of medicine and magic, astronomy and astrology, the art of irrigation and its influence on the garden, and the symbolic connection between pleasure gardens and the Garden of Eden, between the sky and architectural domes and on traditional cosmology and its connection to religion. Today, the hexagram is known as the 'Star of David' and is seen as the definitive symbol of Judaism; the term is even used in Islamic countries. There is a degree of confusion about its origins, name and associations. In Europe, the pentagram is usually known as King Solomon's Seal, while the hexagram is known as the Star of David; and it is often assumed that this was always the case. However, the evidence points to the gradual evolution of the hexagram from a Roman cosmological symbol to a religious and magical symbol which was not specifically connected to one religion or people. Research suggests that both motifs were used by different religions and that the clearest meaning of the hexagram is associated with magical techniques to ward off evil forces."

10

13th Degree
The Royal Arch of Solomon

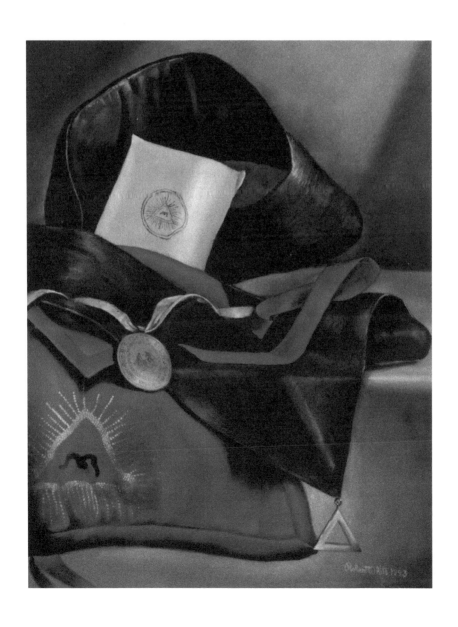

Kabbalists believe the universe began with a benevolent sacrifice by God. Unlike Christianity, which says God sacrificed his only son to save the world, Kabbalah teaches that God sacrificed himself so that the world and the human race might flourish. Kabbalists describe God's sacrifice as tsimtsum, the Hebrew word for "withdrawal." Kabbalists believe God existed in the form of pure energy in the time before creation. The power of God's energy was so vast that it prevented anything else from existing in the universe. To make room for the human race and everything else in the universe, God first had to recoil into itself. In the process of withdrawal, God's identity shattered, dispersing God's energy throughout the universe. Aspects of God, in the form of the ten sefirot, then descended through time and space into the newly created world of material reality—the world in which humans live. Every kabbalist's main duty is tikkun, the process of restoring Kabbalah's fractured God to a state of wholeness through righteousness and good deeds.

Major motifs in Freemasonry include the building of King Solomon's Temple, the search for light, and the lost word of a Master Mason. The temple and the ability of the high priest to pronounce the name of God properly while in the Holy of Holies comprised much of the substantive nature of the Jewish High Holy days of worship in ancient times. The activities of the high priest within the Sanctum Sanctorum are particularly featured in the Royal Arch Degree. There is no doubt that there is a confluence between Freemasonry and the ancient Hebrew religion. This present study seeks to establish that there is a parallel between certain themes from the Kabbalah and Freemasonry. This thesis will be developed by examining the works of authors devoted to the Kabbalah and comparing them with the degrees and lectures of Freemasonry. Gershom G. Scholem in his book, *On the Kabbalah and Its Symbolism*, asserts that "Kabbalistic speculation and doctrine is concerned with the realm of the divine emanations or Sefiroth, in which God's creative power unfolds" (Scholem, 1965). Scholem contends that the Kabbalist speaks about spheres of light and divine names, and that God's name is the highest concentration of divine power. This concern with God's name and the function of light correlates with the activities of the high priest in the ancient temple and with some of the substance of the masonic degrees and lectures. Charles Ponce in his book, *Kabbalah,* asserts that the Sefiroth and En-Sof are two major concepts in the Kabbalah. The En-Sof can be translated to read "without end." This term is the name of God in the Kabbalah. Both Ponce and Scholem contend that the En-Sof and its emanations, the Sefiroth, are inseparable. Ponce describes the Sefiroth as being ten points of light which develop from the En-Sof. This light makes the world comprehensible to man. The concept of light and its effect on the work of Freemasonry is a critical component of all masonic degrees. Ponce examines the beliefs of some Kabbalists who maintain that the light emanating from the En-Sof was not reflected in the Sefiroth but in the body of Adam Kadmon. Adam Kadmon represents the body of heavenly or primordial man. The Sefiroth are then portions or parts of the heavenly man's body. The Kabbalists believe that the spiritual portions of any man can contain the Sefiroth. The challenge is for man to restore and establish the Sefiroth in his spiritual life. Consequently, mortal man can be united with divine man. At the heart of Freemasonry and its masonic precepts is the encouragement and inculcation of values which can "Make good men better." Faith, hope, and charity and values such as fortitude, prudence, temperance, and justice are the cornerstones of masonic conduct and comprise many of the fundamental precepts of Freemasonry (see attached illustration at the end of this file from Gershom G. Scholem's book, *On the Kabbalah and its Symbolism)*. Wisdom, strength, and beauty are the foundations of the masonic lodge, and in fact, beauty, with which the Freemason is taught to adorn all important undertakings, is at the very center of the Sefiroth. Furthermore, the Sefiroth of strength is found on the left-hand side of all the Sefirot, which corresponds to the placement of one of the pillars in the masonic lodge.

The Kabbaiists believe that the transmission of the name of God from master to pupil is part of the rites of initiation. The newly raised brother also receives a word in a certain manner, which is never used in normal conversation. Masonically, the ability of a freemason to recite the word and reproduce it as it was given to him are the identifying characteristics of a Master Mason. The Kabbalists believe that air, water, and fire were used to create the world. The Hebrew letter, Mem, belongs to the class of Mutes, according to Ponce. These letters do not have any sound in their production. The letter, Mem, is associated with water, and since the fish is the chief occupant of water, it is silent as well. The newly raised freemason is instructed about a particular word which is whispered to another brother. This "muted" word begins with the letter M, which corresponds with the letter, Mem. The Kabbalists also believe that the earth was created from water, which is related to the dirt of Hiram's burial site. Therefore, the word used in raising a Freemason has the characteristic of being earthlike.

There are two different perspectives about the Kabbalistic roots for Freemasonry. The first being religious people condemning Freemasonry, Judaism, and the Kabbalah as being anti-Christian and often equating the whole

with Satanism. "Freemasonry and the New World Order are Nazism revived.";
"…that one key ritual in freemasonry involves drinking from human skulls….";
and "Freemasonry is the instrument created to carry out this return to paganism." Albert Pike's *Morals and Dogma*: "all the Masonic associations owe to
it their Secrets and their Symbols." Some claim that Freemasonry is divided
into two branches. "There is a branch of the Scottish Rite and the branch of
the Shriners. Scottish Freemasonry is the Christian branch while the Shriners
are actually the Islamic branch." The second is composed of Freemasons and
Kabbalists who promote the theory of Freemasonry's link to the Kabbalah.
They are entitled to their opinions, but it must be stressed that they do not
speak for Freemasonry. They are only expressing their opinions. They view the
study of both as enhancing their relationship with God.

Furthermore, three rules comprise the Kabbalistic views, which are based
on honor and duty, the three types of fear. We tend to think of fear as a negative emotion, the source of anxiety and discouragement. Kabbalah instead
presents fear as the primary motivator of every righteous thought and deed in
the universe. To understand this surprising portrayal of fear, we need to understand the three types of fear described in the Zohar, Kabbalah's main text.
The first type of fear involves the things we hold dear in our lives on earth: our
home, our health, our friends, and our possessions. Fearing the loss of any of
the above does not qualify as fear in Kabbalah. Similarly, Kabbalah considers
fear of damnation, or any type of consequence in the afterlife, an unacceptable
application of the concept of fear. Kabbalah refers to fear of loss in the material world and in the world hereafter as "evil fear." The third type of fear is the
only fear kabbalists must honor and cultivate, and that's the fear of God. In the
Essential Zohar, Berg insists that kabbalists replace the word "fear" with "awe"
in describing the emotion they should feel when contemplating God. Though
"fear of God" appears in the Old Testament and in the Zohar, Berg believes the
phrase was intended to convey a feeling of respect and admiration, not worry
or concern. Awe in the face of God, the third fear described in the Zohar, is the
most powerful gift God gives us. It is the awareness that God is the source of all
the energy, wisdom, and strength in the universe. Berg views this awareness as
the key to kabbalistic faith, the beacon that keeps followers loyal to their only
goal: bridging the gap between the perfect world that God initially created and
the broken world that human beings inherited after God withdrew. By always
remaining in awe of God's power and self-sacrifice, kabbalists should never
indulge in doubt or self-pity. Instead, they should draw inspiration from God's
power and achievement and strive to honor God by restoring its wholeness.

11

14th Degree
Perfect Elu

Before I begin my initial discussions on the 14th degree – The Perfect Elu, there are many things that catch my attention as well as an overlapping theme that is correlated with the following ideas of Masonry. With the basis of Freemasonry and the attention it gives to detail, symbolism, and in this case, perfection, once again shows how basic everyday things can be correlated into every Mason's life. In this degree, Perfect Elu means to justify the duties of every Mason further than what we know from previous degrees. This degree means to teach every Mason that the duties of a man should be followed with the careful undergoing of many obligations. Although my discussion will cover the idea of perfection, it is vital for me to give some background info.

In the 14th degree, it is in the qualifications of every Mason to follow the duties required. These are that every Mason should assist, encourage, and defend the brethren. This idea is similar to many of the ideas in past degrees, which I will discuss in a later chapter. Furthermore, every Mason should protect the oppressed, especially fellow Masons, but they should also relieve oneself from want and distresses. It is said that through the enlightenment of the people, we shall better our lives at a slow yet steady pace.

And lastly, this degree stresses the service of common good and how every Mason should be fruitful of all good works. With these duties in mind, I have noticed a basic general meaning to how every degree can be related to another. And, with this idea in mind, I have come to notice that the 14th degree stresses the concept of perfection, how it's obtained, where it comes from, and how it can be manifested through various aspects of one's life. The idea of perfection, before reading through the degree, was shown through the idea of how every Mason should be consistent. This idea of consistency is something that has been relevant throughout my studies of the degrees. In this chapter, the idea of perfection is filled with much symbolic reasoning, and through that, we can notice a trend.

Perfection is something that comes from the perfect Elus. These rules are applicable in every Mason's life; they are meant to be both bound and free, setting equilibrium. These ideas come from the idea that we should be bound by our obligation and free from prejudice, intolerance, and envy. This idea comes into play again on similar levels with the idea that authority and liberty play hand-in-hand in our equilibrium. Furthermore, this degree is styled to represent the perfection and completion of the degrees in the Scottish Rite Symbolic Lodge, which is very similar and often compared to that of the 13th degree, for it shows how every Mason should be consistent and be perfect in that we should complete what we start and have it play roles in our lives that overtake any other important concepts that Masons should hold deep in our thoughts and lives. This signifies the contrast between the crypts of Enoch and that of Solomon.

These crypts, built by both Enoch and Solomon, are meant to correlate with one another. The first crypts are inward symbols, meaning that they are being hidden under the earth so that they directly tend for us to focus our relations upon the inward qualities of a man; this is a reminder of the Symbolic Lodge instruction that is the internal and not the external. These, again, are qualities that are recommended for a man to be made into a Mason.

The second crypt was built differently than that of the first but was built this way for a common purpose. In a very different fashion, the crypts must be seen as distinct yet united and unified symbols. These are distinct because each has its very own meaning that differs from the other, but they are united because together, they form an entirely different symbol with its own interpretation. The crypt of Enoch was built vertically, and this vertical direction is symbolic as well and stands for the spiritual dimension of the universe.

When Enoch was directed to build his crypt and deposit the sacred treasure therein, the completion of this led to him not suffering death but being sent directly to heaven for his duties. The treasure was then taken to Solomon, who deposited it into his own crypt, which was built horizontally between his most retired apartments of the Sanctum Sanatorium of the Temple. The horizontal direction signifies earthly things. Solomon was not a spiritual leader; his wisdom was the wisdom of the earth—he was a wise and just ruler of men but less so of himself. Uniting the vertical crypt that of Enoch and the horizontal crypt of Solomon creates the symbol of the cross (+). This idea of the cross simply shows the united spiritual and earthly qualities that should be united in man, and two equally important aspects playing a vital role in one's life is the basis of providing the model of perfection for this degree. This is the perfection that is taught to every Mason: Living this life to the fullest while preparing for the next.

These ideas that derive from the 14th degree and how it relates to Masons' triumph to live life to the fullest. They highlight that under perfection is something that is a constant struggle. It is always attainable and comes from the aspects in our lives (previously discussed) that have to do with who we are as Men and how this is manifested through the things we do in our lives. We are taught as Masons that we are constantly being examined for out duties and roles in our lives. With the celebration of the revelation of the 13th degree comes the examination of the 14th, the perfection in our lives. These aspects are taught to show the significance of "knowledge without its application is of little or no value." With knowledge comes responsibility, and one must prove themselves worthy to possess it. The mere position of knowledge plays little role, and for that, it is not seen as a virtue. Without its application and effect it can have in our lives, it can mean nothing. Yet let it be known that knowledge when it is properly applied can result in the wisdom of man; this comes from the Book of Proverbs that says that knowledge was coexistent with creation.

With the ideas of perfection in mind, as well as how key symbolism is used to signify its meaning in our lives, it is evident that there was some sort of idea of being perfect that bled into the important ideas built around Freemasonry. An important symbol in this degree is the seal of Solomon. It is formed by two interlaced triangles, one white and the other black. Firstly, the colors of black and white are recognized for their consistency and ideas of perfection; the two colors chosen are the lightest of lights and the darkest of darks (white vs. black). These show how there are aspects in our lives that play roles in the creation of who we are by what we do. This correlation between two things is the everyday role of Masons to be aware of, the constant struggle of doing what we are meant to do with purpose. Furthermore, there is a six-pointed star that can be found hidden in Pythagorean tetractys. Among the Greeks, the hexad (or number 6) was considered a symbol of marriage, and the figure drawn from the six dots that circle the central dot of the tetractys form an apt symbol of this number, as it creates six smaller equilateral triangles, the children of the union of the two large triangles. The deeper and more significant meanings are yet to be revealed till later degrees, but one major theme I have noticed is how perfection can be seen done through consistency, as previously stated. Merely, it can be seen that every symbol has significance because of the idea of perfection, the use of the triangle, the number six, or marriage. These ideas are very perfect in the sense that they are meaningful toward aspects we all should possess. We know that the triangle is three-pointed and equilateral, and we further know how the seal of Solomon consists of three equal triangles. Although, this may be an observation not seen as too relevant; it became evident that this degree is correlated with perfection, so as I stated in my introduction, there has been an overlapping theme that has shown importance: That every aspect in a Mason's life should be based on the idea that we should be fruitful in all our works, assuming we all should strive to be perfect. Although perfection may be subjective or unattainable, that is the point. I believe it is vital to let every Mason know that life is never perfect; we are "dealt the cards we get," and with that we have to make the best of it. That means never giving up and always remembering the ideas, themes, and morally correct aspects that every Mason should have present in their lives. It's not the idea of perfection we need to strive for—it's the idea to strive for everything in life, and through this striving we should never give up on making our lives better, and through this... perfection will come.

12

I n the fifteenth degree – The Knight of the East or of the Sword, there are major points of reason that aim to portray many of the lessons, like the ones we have previously learned. And, like the other degrees in Masonry, it is filled with symbols, and we are meant to use and understand these symbols for one chief purpose: to teach us the leading lesson of this degree that relates fidelity to obligation and constancy and perseverance under difficulties and discouragement, something every Mason must achieve. There are loads of spiritual values that are incorporated with this degree that overlap with the idea of Masonry as a whole and its journey. It is said that Masonry is in a crusade against ignorance, intolerance, fanaticism, superstition, uncharitableness, and error. These ideas are vital for every Mason to hold close to their hearts. I believe it would be in the duty of every Mason to act as Masonry itself has acted; as a boat that does not sail with the trade winds, a smooth sea, and with a steady free breeze but more likely meeting and overcoming opposing currents, harsh winds, and slowly dead calms. This is just as life will always throw obstacles in many people's journeys, never acting calm, always giving us the opportunity to prove ourselves and overcome certain obstacles in our path. With that in mind, I believe that this degree is meaning to teach us that we must always act as the Masonry Boat (so to speak)—always overcoming everything that lies in our path, never folding under any pressure, and knowing that with the crew's best interest in mind, they must overcome hard hurdles, for life will never be easy because if it were easy, then everyone would be in their ideal situation, which is never usually the case.

Further, just as Masonry has acted upon itself for its own success, we must do the same. Masonry has overcome her chief obstacles that led to her success, which are the apathy and faithlessness of her own selfish children and the supine indifference of the world. The first lesson that one learns, who engages in any great work of reform or beneficence, is that men are essentially careless, something we all must know, and indifferent as to everything that does not concern their own personal and immediate welfare. It is to single men, and not to the united efforts of many, that all the great works done by man, struggling toward perfection, are owed. For example, an enthusiast who imagines that he can inspire with his own enthusiasm the multitude that eddies around him, or even the few who have associated themselves with him as co-workers, is grievously mistaken, and most often the conviction of his own mistake is followed by discouragement and disgust. According to Albert Pike's *Morals and Dogma*, he who endeavors to serve, to benefit, and improve the world is like a swimmer, who struggles against a rapid current, in a river lashed into angry waves by the winds. Often, they roar over his head, often they beat him back and baffle him. Most men yield to the stress of the current and float with it to the shore, or are swept over the rapids; and only here and there, the stout, strong heart and vigorous arms struggle on toward ultimate success.

These are some of the moral dilemmas we are constantly faced with, but now with our newfound knowledge, we can do everything within our power to help ourselves and the ones around us in order to use these spiritual values. Nonetheless, we should consider the motionless stationary that most frets and impedes the current of progress, meaning we must always know to continue on our journey, never letting anything come between that. At the very least, we should know that the Masons that doubt and hesitate and are discouraged; that disbelieve in the capability of man to improve; that are not disposed to toil and labor for the interest and well-being of general humanity; that expect others to do all, even of that which they do not oppose or ridicule; which they sit, applauding and doing nothing, or perhaps prognosticating failure. It is a chief value for every Mason to never settle for failure, for it should not be associated with us in any way, for it should never be a settlement of any sort.

We are taught to leave those who are discouraged, engaged in the good work, and knowing whenever to us, as to them, success is always uncertain, remote, and contingent. We must always still remember that the only question for us to ask, as true men and as true Masons, is, "What does our duty require us to do?" We should never ask what will be the result and the reward if we do our duty. Work on, the Sword in one hand, and the trowel in the other! This is one of the vital lessons of this degree. Masonry teaches that God is a Paternal being, who has an interest in his creatures, such as is expressed in the title Father; an interest unknown to all the systems of Paganism, untaught in all the theories of philosophy; an interest not only in the glorious beings of other spheres, the sons of light, the dwellers in Heavenly worlds, but in us, poor, ignorant, and unworthy; that He has pity for the erring, pardon for the guilty, love for the pure, knowledge for the humble, and promises of immortal life for those who trust in him and obey him. By saying this, Albert Pike aims to teach Masons that God has our best interests at heart and we must do everything within our power to avoid becoming ignorant or acting in any unworthy way; we must earnestly win over all we set out to achieve. This acts as another chief value that is set out, not only by this degree, but Masonry as a whole. In addition, we must always have our faith in Him. Without a belief in him, life is miserable; the world would seem much darker, the universe disrobed of its splendors, the intellectual tie to nature would be broken, the charm of existence would slowly dissolve, the great hope of being lost; something every Mason must avoid. From *Morals and Dogma* and *A Bridge to Light,* we learned and now know that Masonry teaches that all of all the events and actions that take place in the universe of worlds and the eternal succession of ages, there is not one, even the minutest, which god did not forever foresee with all the distinctness of immediate vision, combining all, so that man's free will should be His instrument, like all the other forces of nature. We must act as an additional force, just as everything else in this world must, but never counteracting nature nor His nature; that way life can set on an even keel.

Another spiritual value inculcated by this degree is that it teaches that the soul of man is formed by Him for a purpose, that built up in its proportions, and fashioned in every part, by infinite skill, an emanation from His spirit, its nature, necessity, and design are virtues. It is so formed, so molded, so fashioned, so exactly balances, so exquisitely proportioned in every part, that sin introduced into it is misery; that vicious thoughts fall upon it like drops of poison; and guilty desires, breathing on its delicate fibers, make plague-spot there, deadly as those of pestilence upon the body. We know this through the words of Albert Pike, and further, that everything must serve as a virtue, just as all of the previous ideas are considered. None should be made for vice, rather for purity, as its end, rest and happiness. Never more vainly would we attempt to reverse the nature of nature's wonders, making the mountain sink to the level of the valley, or waves of angry sea turning back into its shores and ceasing to thunder upon the beach.

Finally, and ultimately, we know that God is good, and that what He does is right. This known, the works of creation, the changes of life, the destinies of eternity, are all spread before us, as the dispensations and counsels of infinite love. This known, we then know that the love of god is working on issues, like itself, beyond all thought and imagination, good and glorious; and that the only reason why we do not understand it yet is that it is too glorious for us to understand. God's love takes care of all, and nothing is neglected. It watches over all, provides for all, makes wise adaptations for all; for age, for infancy, for maturity, for childhood; in every scene of this or another world; for want, weakness, joy, sorrow, and even for sin. All is good and well and right; and shall be so forever. Then that which causes us trials shall yield us triumph; and that which made our heart ache shall fill us with gladness; and we shall then feel that there, as here, the only true happiness is to LEARN, to advance, and to improve; which could not happen unless we had filled it and commenced with error, ignorance, and imperfection. We must pass through the darkness to reach the light.

13

16th Degree
Prince of Jerusalem

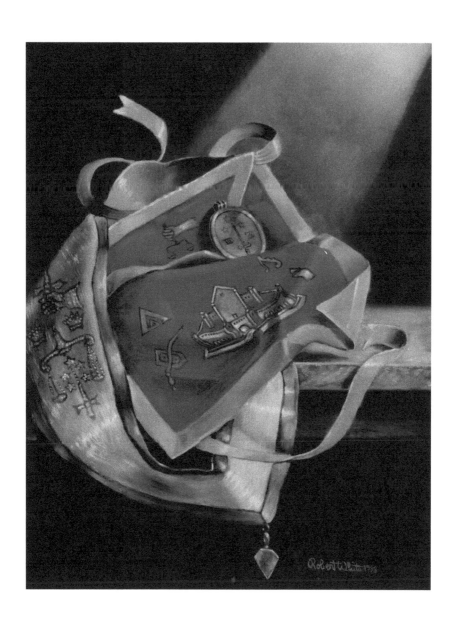

Albert Pike, in *Morals and Dogma*, spends a lot of time speaking about righteousness and has a firm belief that the whole world as well as every upright heart is God's temple. By this, he means to establish that there is a reign, and by this, only God can judge. By this system he believes that it is vital, according to the New Law, that we must rule the reigns of love, peace, charity, and toleration, just as it was needed to rebuild the temple. Quite simply, Pike says, "Execute true judgment; and show mercy and compassion every man to his brother. Oppress not the widow nor the fatherless, the stranger nor the poor; and let none of you imagine evil against his brother in his heart. Speak ye every man the truth to his neighbor; execute the judgment of Truth and Peace in your gates; and love no false oath; for all these I hate, saith the Lord.

"According to the basic idea of the 'rules of righteousness,' we must let those who have power rule in righteousness, and Princes in judgment. And let him that is a judge be as a hiding-place from the wind, and a covert from the tempest; as rivers of water in a dry place; as the shadow of a great rock in a weary land. Then the vile person shall no longer be called liberal; nor the churl bountiful; and the work of justice shall be peace; and the effect of justice, peace and security; and wisdom and knowledge shall be the stability of the times. Walk ye righteously and speak uprightly; despise the gains of oppression, shake from your hands the contamination of bribes; stop not your ears against the cries of the oppressed, nor shut your eyes that you may not see the crimes of the great; and you shall dwell on high, and your place of defense be like munitions of rocks."

These words by Pike are the foundation of how he feels that God is the center of everything and only by his standards can we judge righteously. As Masons, we must not forget these precepts of the Old Law; and especially do not forget, as we advance, that every Mason, however humble, is a brother, and the laboring man a peer. We must remember always that all Masonry is work, and that the trowel is an emblem of the Degrees in this Council. Labor, when rightly understood, is both noble and ennobling, and intended to develop man's moral and spiritual nature, and not to be deemed a disgrace or a misfortune. Everything around us is, in its bearings and influences, moral. This meaning to Pike was extremely important; this idea focused on the fact that we all have the ability to act righteous.

Nonetheless, Pike also believes that labor is vital in everyday life, for it may have the ability to teach us something, just as Masonry with its great truths. Pike remarks how a life of labor should never be considered as a state of inferiority or degradation. Believing that the Almighty has given us nothing to perform rather than rise up and eat and to lay down and rest is not an ideal mindset. This idea is key; this is believing in the notion that the Almighty has ordained that work shall be done in all the dwellings of life. This also comes with the belief that this is something He has done because it has pleased Him to give man a nature destined to higher ends than indolent repose and irresponsible profitless indulgence; and because, for developing the energies of such a nature, he considers, work is the necessary and proper element, falling into what righteousness means to Pike.

All the relations of life, those of parent, child, brother, sister, friend, associate, lover and beloved, husband, wife, are moral, throughout every living tie and thrilling nerve that binds them together. Pike believes they cannot subsist a day nor an hour without putting the mind to a trial of its truth, fidelity, forbearance, and disinterestedness. Pike claims that "A great city is one extended scene of moral action." There is a blow struck in it, but it has a purpose, ultimately good or bad, and therefore moral. There is no action performed, but has a motive, and motives are the special jurisdiction of morality. As an example, Pike remarked how equipages, houses, and furniture are symbols of what is moral, and they in a thousand ways minister to right or wrong feelings. Everything that belongs to us, ministering to our comfort or luxury, awakens in us emotions of pride or gratitude, of selfishness or vanity; thoughts of self-indulgence or merciful remembrances of the needy and the destitute. Everything acts upon and influences us. God's great law of sympathy and harmony is as potent and inflexible as His law of gravitation. A sentence embodying a noble thought stirs our blood; a noise made by a child frets and exasperates us and influences our actions.

Righteousness is in our everyday lives and can often reflect the kind of people we are. This is something Pike believes in sternly and often takes it beyond any explanation. There is always a conflict, and there will always be problems, for we are only human. For us to achieve perfection, it will always be an uphill struggle. But with God in our hearts and minds, we can do what it is to the best of our ability and act as often as possible according to the words given to us by the teachings of Masonry and through great teachers such as Albert Pike, who was very spiritual and often saw that objects, influences, and relations lie around us all and further believing we all deem it to be so. But he only lives a charmed life, he says, like that of genius and poetic inspirations, who communes with the spiritual scene around him. We can hear the voice of the spirit in every sound, according to Pike, seeing its signs in every passing form of things, and feeling its impulse in all action, passion, and being.

Being spiritual has had a huge effect on Albert Pike's belief in the importance of righteousness. It is often said that mines of wisdom always lay very near to us, unsuspected lessons that are constant around us. According to Pike, righteousness goes beyond the actual act of being righteous, or what we feel is that act. Pike discusses that the great problem with humanity is wrought out in the humblest abodes; no more than this is done in the highest. This is pertaining to the human heart, and as Pike would agree, the beauty of love, the charm of Friendship, the sacredness of Sorrow, the heroism of Patience, the noble self-sacrifice, these and their like, alone, make life to be life indeed and are its grandeur and its power. These are the priceless treasures and glory of humanity that Pike is speaking about; he feels that they are not things of condition and all places and all scenes are like clothes with the greater chard of virtues.

In closing, Pike urges us to never forget these precepts of the old law, and especially not to forget, as you advance, that every Mason, however humble, is your brother, and the laboring man your peer. Even never really knowing what it means to be righteous doesn't mean we cannot strive for the act of wanting to learn and never giving up on that. Also, we must always remember that all Masonry is work. We must remember that labor should be understood; that it can be noble and ennobling; its intentions are never to be forgotten, and they are intended to develop our moral and spiritual nature, which from earlier discussions is vital for our acts of righteousness. Pike, during his discussion, describes the serene and bright morning when we recover our conscious existence from the embraces of sleep; when, from that image of Death God calls us to a new life, and again gives us existence, and His mercies visit us in every bright ray and glad thought, and call for gratitude and content; the silence of that early dawn, the hushed silence, as it were, of expectation; the holy eventide, its cooling breeze, its lengthening shadows, its falling shades, it's still and sober hour; the sultry noontide and the stern and solemn midnight; and Spring-time, and chastening Autumn; and Summer, that unbars our gates, and carries us forth amidst the ever renewed wonders of the world; and Winter, that gathers us around the evening hearth—all these, as they pass, touch by turns the springs of the spiritual life in us, and are conducting that life to good or evil. The idle watch-hand often points to something within us; and the shadow of the gnomon on the dial often falls upon the conscience. Ultimately, Pike can never fully answer that there are "rules in righteousness" when we cannot fully understand its meaning, yet the mere act of being righteous more likely spells out the rules as well as moral guidelines, for it has a lot of deeper meaning and calls out for our inner self, and this is something that must comprise our moral foundation.

14

17th Degree
Knight of the East and West

The 17th degree, Knight of the East and West, contains spiritual power from which the 15th and 16th degree are the raw force. Generally speaking, the 17th degree has reiterated that only God is wise. The wisdom of man is but the reflection and image of that of God. He is the Father, and His WISDOM the mother of creation: for He united Himself with WISDOM (Sophia) and communicated to it the germ of creation and it brought forth the material world. He created the ideal world only and caused the material world to be made real after its type by His LOGOS, which is His speech, and at the same time the Idea of Ideas, the Intellectual World.

The Word is not only the Creator but occupies the place of the Supreme Being. Through Him all the Powers and Attributes of God act. On the other side, as the first representative of the Human Family, He is the Protector of men and their Shepherd. God gives to man the Soul or intelligence, which exists before the body, and which he unites with the body. The reasoning principle comes from God through the Word and communes with God and with the Word, but there is also in man an irrational Principle, that of the inclinations and passions that they produce.

Disorder, emanates from inferior spirits who fill the air as ministers of God. The body, taken from the Earth, and the irrational Principle that animates it concurrent with the rational.

Principles are hated by God, while the rational soul that He has given it, is, as it were, is captive in this prison, this coffin, that encompasses it. The present condition of man is not his primitive condition, when he was the image of the Logos. He has fallen from his first estate. But he may raise himself again, by following the directions of WISDOM and of the Angels, which God has commissioned to aid him in freeing himself from the bonds of the body, and combating Evil, the existence whereof God has permitted, to furnish him the means of exercising his liberty. The souls that are purified, not by the Law but by light, rise to the Heavenly regions, to enjoy there a perfect felicity. Those that persevere in evil go from body to body, the seats of passions and evil desires. The familiar lineaments of these doctrines will be recognized by all who read the Epistles of St. Paul, who wrote after Philo, the latter living till the reign of Caligula and being the contemporary of Christ.

Furthermore, Masons should be familiar with the Doctrine (dubbed applicable to daily life): that the Supreme Being is a centre of Light whose rays are emanations pervade the Universe; for that is the Light for which all Masonic journeys are a search, and of which the sun and moon in our Lodges are only emblems: that Light and Darkness, chief enemies from the beginning of Time, dispute with each other the empire of the world; which we symbolize by the candidate wandering in darkness and being brought to light: that the world was created, not by the Supreme Being, but by a secondary agent, who is but His WORD, and by types which are but his ideas, aided by an INTELLIGENCE, or WISDOM, which gives one of His Attributes; in which we see the occult meaning of the necessity of recovering "the Word;" and of our two columns of STRENGTH and WISDOM, which are also the two parallel lines that bound the circle representing the Universe: that the visible world is the image of the invisible world; that the essence of the Human Soul is the image of God, and it existed before the body; that the object of its terrestrial life is to disengage itself of its body or its sepulchre; and that it will ascend to the Heavenly regions whenever it shall be purified; in which we see the meaning, now almost forgotten in our Lodges, of the mode of preparation of the candidate for apprenticeship, and his tests and purifications in the first Degree, according to the Ancient and Accepted Scottish Rite.

Importantly, The Ram was His living symbol; which you see reproduced in this Degree, lying on the book with seven seals on the tracing-board. He caused the creation of the world by the Primitive Thought (Ennoia), or Spirit (Pneuma), that issued from him by means of his Voice or the WORD; and which Thought or Spirit was personified as the Goddess NEITH. She, too, was a divinity of Light, and mother of the Sun; and the Feast of Lamps was celebrated in her honor at Sais. The Creative Power, another manifestation of Deity, proceeding to the creation conceived of in her, the Divine Intelligence, produced with its Word the Universe, symbolized by an egg issuing from the mouth of KNEPH; from which egg came PHTHA, image of the Supreme Intelligence as realized in the world, and the type of that manifested in man; the principal agent, also, of Nature, or the creative and productive Fire. PHRE or RS, the Sun, or Celestial Light, whose symbol was the point within a circle, was the son of PHTHA; and TIPHE, his wife, or the celestial firmament, with the seven celestial bodies, animated by spirits of genii that govern them, was represented on many of the monuments, clad in blue or yellow, her garments sprinkled with stars, and accompanied by the sun, moon, and five planets; and she was the type of Wisdom, and they of the Seven Planetary Spirits of the Gnostics, that with her presided over and governed the sublunary world.

In this Degree, unknown for a hundred years to those who have practiced it, these emblems reproduced refer to these old doctrines. The lamb, the yellow hangings strewed with stars, the seven columns, candlesticks, and seals all recall them to us. The Lion was the symbol of ATUM-RE, the Great God of Upper

Egypt; the Hawk, of RA or PHRE; the Eagle, of ENDES; the Bull, of APIS; and three of these are seen under the platform on which our altar stands. The first HERMES was the INTELLIGENCE, or WORD of God. Moved with compassion for a race living without law, and wishing to teach them that they sprang from His bosom, and to point out to them the way that they should go (the books that the first Hermes, the same with Enoch, had written on the mysteries of divine science, in the sacred characters, being unknown to those who lived after the flood). God sent to man OSIRIS and ISIS, accompanied by THOTH, the incarnation or terrestrial repetition of the first Hermes, who taught men the arts, science, and the ceremonies of religion and then ascended to Heaven or the Moon. OSIRIS was the Principle of Good. TYPHON, like AHRIMAN, was the principle and source of all that is evil in the moral and physical order. Like the Satan of Gnosticism, he was confounded with Matter. From Egypt or Persia, the new Platonists borrowed the idea, and the Gnostics received it from them, that man, in his terrestrial career, is successively under the influence of the Moon, of Mercury, of Venus, of the Sun, of Mars, of Jupiter, and of Saturn, until he finally reaches the Elysian Fields; an idea again symbolized in the Seven Seals.

To some, the world was created by the LOGOS or WORD, the first manifestation of, or emanation from, the Deity. To others, the beginning of creation was by the emanation of a ray of Light, creating the principle of Light and Life. The Primitive THOUGHT, creating the inferior Deities, a succession of INTELLIGENCES, the Iynges of Zoroaster, his Amshaspands, Izeds, and Ferouers, the Ideas of Plato, the Aeons of the Gnostics, the Angels of the Jews, the Nous, the Demiourgos, the DIVINE REASON, the Powers or Forces of Philo, and the Alohayim, Forces or Superior Gods of the ancient legend with which Genesis begins, to these and other intermediaries the creation was owing. No restraints were laid on the Fancy and the Imagination. The veriest Abstractions became Existences and Realities. The attributes of God, personified, became Powers, Spirits, and Intelligences. God was the Light of Light, Divine Fire, and the Abstract Intellectuality, the Root or Germ of the Universe. Simon Magus, founder of the Gnostic faith, and many of the early Judaizing Christians, admitted that the manifestations of the Supreme Being, as FATHER, or JEHOVAH, SON or CHRIST, and HOLY SPIRIT, were only so many different modes of Existence, or Forces of the same God. To others they were, as were the multitude of Subordinate Intelligences, rcal and distinct beings.

In the Talmud, every star, every country, every town, and almost every tongue has a Prince of Heaven as its Protector. JEHUEL is the guardian of fire, and MICHAEL of water. Seven spirits assist each; those of fire being Seraphiel, Gabriel, Nitriel, Tammael, Tchimschiel, Hadarniel, and Sarniel. These seven are represented by the square columns of this Degree, while the columns JACHIN and BOAZ represent the angels of fire and water. But the columns are not representatives of these alone. To Basilides, God was without name, uncreated, at first containing and concealing in Himself the Plenitude of His Perfections; and when these are by Him displayed and manifested, there result as many particular Existences, all analogous to Him, and still and always Him. To the Essenes and the Gnostics, the East and the West both devised this faith; that the Ideas, Conceptions, or Manifestations of the Deity were so many Creations, so many Beings, all God, nothing without Him, but more than what we now understand by the word ideas. They emanated from and were again merged in God. They had a kind of middle existence between our modern ideas, and the intelligences or ideas, elevated to the rank of genii, of the Oriental mythology.

With the Ophites, a sect of the Gnostics, there were seven inferior spirits (inferior to Ialdabaoth, the Demiourgos or Actual Creator: Michael, Suriel, Raphael, Gabriel, Thauthabaoth, Erataoth, and Athaniel, the genii of the stars called the Bull, the Dog, the Lion, the Bear, the Serpent, the Eagle, and the Ass that formerly figured in the constellation Cancer, and symbolized respectively by those animals, as Ialdabaoth, Iao, Adonai, Eloi, Orai, and Astaphai were the genii of Saturn, the Moon, the Sun, Jupiter, Venus, and Mercury. The WORD appears in all these creeds. It is the Ormuzd of Zoroaster, the Ainsoph of the Kabbalah, the Nous of Platonism and Philonism, and the Sophia or Demiourgos of the Gnostics. And all these creeds, while admitting these different manifestations of the Supreme Being, held that His identity was immutable and permanent. That was Plato's distinction between the Being always the same and the perpetual flow of things incessantly changing, the Genesis. The belief in dualism in some shape was universal. Those who held that everything emanated from God, aspired to God, and re-entered into God believed that among those emanations were two adverse Principles, of Light and Darkness and Good and Evil. This prevailed in Central Asia and in Syria, while in Egypt it assumed the form of Greek speculation. In the former, a second Intellectual Principle was admitted, active in its Empire of Darkness, audacious against the Empire of Light. So the Persians and Sabeans understood it. In Egypt, this second Principle was Matter, as the word was used by the Platonic School, with its sad attributes, Vacuity, Darkness, and Death. In their theory, matter could be animated only by the low communication of a principle of divine life. It resists the influences that would spiritualize it. That resisting Power is Satan, the rebellious Matter, and Matter that does not partake of God.

Behold the object, the end, the result of the great speculations and logomachies of antiquity; the ultimate annihilation of evil, and restoration of Man to his first estate, by a Redeemer, a Masayah, Christos, the incarnate Word, Reason, or Power of Deity. This Redeemer is the Word or Logos, the Ormuzd of Zoroaster, the Ain soph of the Kabbalah, the Nous of Platonism and Philonism; He that was in the Beginning with God, and was God, and by whom everything was made. That He was looked for by all the People of the East is abundantly shown by the Gospel of John and the Letters of Paul; wherein scarcely anything seemed necessary to be said in proof that such a Redeemer was to come; but all the energies of the writers are devoted to showing that Jesus was that Christos whom all the nations were expecting; the "Word," the Masayah, the Anointed or Consecrated One.

In this Degree, the great contest between good and evil, in anticipation of the appearance and advent of the Word or Redeemer, is symbolized, and the mysterious esoteric teachings of the Essenes and the Cabalists. Of the practices of the former we gain but glimpses in the ancient writers; but we know that, as their doctrines were taught by John the Baptist, they greatly resembled those of greater purity and more nearly perfect, taught by Jesus; and that not only Palestine was full of John's disciples, so that the Priests and Pharisees did not dare to deny John's inspiration; but his doctrine had extended to Asia Minor, and had made converts in luxurious Ephesus, as it also had in Alexandria in Egypt; and that they readily embraced the Christian faith, of which they had before not even heard.

But Masonry still survives, vigorous and strong, as when philosophy was taught in the schools of Alexandria and under the Portico, teaching the same old truths as the Essenes taught by the shores of the Dead Sea, and as John the Baptist preached in the Desert; truths imperishable as the Deity, and undeniable as Light. Those truths were gathered by the Essenes from the doctrines of the Orient and the Occident, from the Zend-Avesta and the Vedas, from Plato and Pythagoras, from India, Persia, Phoenicia, and Syria, from Greece and Egypt, and from the Holy Books of the Jews. Hence, we are called Knights of the East and West, because their doctrines came from both. And with these doctrines, the wheat sifted from the chaff, the Truth separated from Error, Masonry has garnered up in her heart of hearts, and through the fires of persecution, and the storms of calamity, has brought them and delivered them unto us. That God is One, immutable, unchangeable, infinitely just and good;

that Light will finally overcome Darkness—Good conquer sEvil, and Truth be victor over Error—these, rejecting all the wild and useless speculations of the Zend-Avesta, the Kabbalah, the Gnostics, and the Schools, are the religion and Philosophy of Masonry. Those speculations and fancies it is useful to study; that knowing in what worthless and unfruitful investigations the mind may engage, you may the more value and appreciate the plain, simple, sublime, universally acknowledged truths, which have in all ages been the Light by which Masons have been guided on their way; the Wisdom and Strength that like imperishable columns have sustained and will continue to sustain its glorious and magnificent Temple.

15

18th Degree
Knight of the Rose Croix

The main purpose of this degree is the forthcoming of the New Law, the Law of Love, proclaimed in unmistakable terms by Jesus of Nazareth after centuries of spiritual and intellectual darkness in the world when the Sacred Word was again lost. After receiving a Supreme message, the Word was brought to the world by the proclamation of the fatherhood of God and the Brotherhood of Man. The Candidate seeks for answers in the stars, and after the discovery of the words Faith, Hope. and Charity, he was then guided by these to find the light and the Word. This Degree contains many symbols, such as the Rose and Cross, to which the cross has been a sacred symbol in many cultures, and the rose was anciently sacred to the sun and to Aurora, Greek goddess of the Dawn. The idea that they represent resurrection and the renewal of life, and therefore immortality, further means that both the cross and the rose symbolizes immortality won by suffering and sorrow.

The Degree of Rose Croix teaches every Mason of the unity, immutability, and goodness of God; the immortality of the Soul; and the ultimate defeat and extinction of evil and wrong and sorrow by a Redeemer or Messiah, who is said to "yet to come, if he has not already appeared" (Gupta, *Resurrection of Tutankhamun*).

To the idea of new meaning that comes with the Word, it replaces the three pillars of the old Temple, Faith (in God, mankind, and man's self), Hope (in the victory over evil, the advancement of Humanity, and a hereafter), and Charity (relieving the wants and tolerance of the errors and faults of others). To be trustful, to be hopeful, to be indulgent; these, in an age of selfishness, of ill opinion of human nature, of harsh and bitter judgment, are the most important Masonic Virtues, and the true supports of every Masonic Temple. And they are the old pillars of the Temple under different names. "For he only is wise who judges others charitably; he only is strong who is hopeful; and there is no beauty like a firm faith in God, our fellows, and our self," claims Pike.

But the Candidate must endure the passage through a setting that has been described as a kind of Milton or Dante concept of Hell. This comes with the notion of Change and how his transformation of his belief is thus the representation of the Great Work of man. Once he emerges into the Chamber of Light, he sees the initials that form the Word and sees a cubical stone turn into a cross with a rose superimposed on it. From then on, he learns of his foolishness, and he is instructed in the New Law, the Law of Love. The central symbolized idea of this degree focuses on the aspect of change and how transformation is done through God, and further, that the transformation of the Cubical stone being transformed into a cross with a rose entails many specific interpretations and can be quite complicated. However, it is all gathered together to ultimately become understood as the change into the New Law.

As Proclaimed by Albert Pike: "The Cross has been a sacred symbol from the earliest Antiquity. It is found upon all the enduring monuments of the world, in Egypt, in Assyria, in Hindostan, in Persia, and on the Buddhist towers of Ireland. Buddha was said to have died upon it. The Druids cut an oak into its shape and held it sacred, and built their temples in that form. Pointing to the four quarters of the world, it was the symbol of universal nature. It was on a cruciform tree, that Chrishna was said to have expired, pierced with arrows. It was revered in Mexico. But its peculiar meaning in this Degree, is that given to it by the Ancient Egyptians. Thoth or Phika is represented on the oldest monuments carrying in his hand the Crux Ansata, or Ankh, [a Tau cross, with a ring or circle over it]. He is so seen on the double tablet of Shufu and Nob Shufu, builders of the greatest of the Pyramids, at Wadi Maghara, in the peninsula of Sinai. It was the hieroglyphic for life, and with a triangle prefixed meant life-giving. To us therefore it is the symbol of Life—of that life that emanated from the Deity, and of that Eternal Life for which we all hope; through our faith in God's infinite goodness.

"Now, which seems to play a far further role in this degree: the ROSE, which was anciently sacred to Aurora and the Sun. It is a symbol of Dawn, of the resurrection of Light and the renewal of life, and therefore of the dawn of the first day, and more particularly of the resurrection: and the Cross and Rose together are therefore hieroglyphically to be read, the Dawn of Eternal Life which all Nations have hoped for by the advent of a Redeemer.

"The Pelican feeding her young is an emblem of the large and bountiful beneficence of Nature, of the Redeemer of fallen man, and of that humanity and charity that ought to distinguish a Knight of this Degree. The Eagle was the living Symbol of the Egyptian God Mendes or Menthra, whom Sesostris-Ramses made one with Amun-Re, the God of Thebes and Upper Egypt, and the representative of the Sun, the word RE meaning Sun or King. The Compass surmounted with a crown signifies that notwithstanding the high rank attained in Masonry by a Knight of the Rose Croix, equity and impartiality are invariably to govern his conduct signifying how the key symbolism of the Rose Criox is further transcribed into a transformation.

Furthermore, to the word INRI, inscribed on the Crux Ansata over the Master's Seat, many meanings have been assigned. In *Morals and Dogma*, Albert Pikes says that "The Christian Initiate reverentially sees in it the initials of the inscription upon the cross on which Christ suffered—Iesus Nazarenus

Rex ludceorum. The sages of Antiquity connected it with one of the greatest secrets of Nature, that of universal regeneration. They interpreted it thus, Igne Natura renovatur integra; [entire nature is renovated by fire]: The Alchemical or Hermetic Masons framed for it this aphorism, Igne nitrum roris invenitur. And the Jesuits are charged with having applied to it this odious axiom, Justum necare reges impios. The four letters are the initials of the Hebrew words that represent the four elements—Iammim, the seas or water; Nour, fire; Rouach, the air, and Iebeschah, the dry earth". How we read it, I "need not repeat to you." The CROSS, X, was the Sign of the Creative Wisdom or Logos, the Son of God. Plato says, "He expressed him upon the Universe in the figure of the letter X. The next Power to the Supreme God was decussated or figured in the shape of a Cross on the Universe." Mithras signed his soldiers on the forehead with a Cross. X is the mark of 600, the mysterious cycle of the Incarnations.

The Degree of Rose is devoted to and symbolizes the final triumph of truth over falsehood, of liberty over slavery, of light over darkness, of life over death, and of good over evil. The great truth it inculcates is, that notwithstanding the existence of Evil, God is infinitely wise, just, and good: that though the affairs of the world proceed by no rule of right and wrong known to us in the narrowness of our views, yet all is right, for it is the work of God; and all evils, all miseries, all misfortunes, are but as drops in the vast current that is sweeping onward, guided by Him, to a great and magnificent result: that, at the appointed time, He will redeem and regenerate the world, and the Principle, the Power, and the existence of Evil will then cease; that this will be brought about by such means and instruments as He chooses to employ; whether by the merits of a Redeemer that has already appeared, or a Messiah that is yet waited for, by an incarnation of Himself, or by an inspired prophet, it does not belong to us as Masons to decide. Let each judge and believe for himself.

In the meantime, we labor to hasten the coming of that day. The morals of antiquity, of the law of Moses and of Christianity, are ours. We recognize every teacher of Morality, every Reformer, as a brother in this great work. The Eagle is to us the symbol of Liberty, the Compasses of Equality, and the Pelican of Humanity: and our order of Fraternity. Laboring for these, with Faith, Hope, and Charity as our armor, we will wait with patience for the final triumph of Good and the complete manifestation of the Word of God. And thus, it can be interpreted similar to the Candidate who emerges into the Chamber of light, and then seeing a cubical stone turning into a cross with the rose, it should be understood as a form of reasoning and learning about how change is good.

16

The Mythic Journey

The central aspect of these degrees shouldn't be seen as different segments but as one whole that entails from beginning to end the very nature that every Mason should possess. Beginning in the fourth degree, The Secret Master, we are taught of Duty, a mission we must and should willfully serve as Masons and agree to serve our fellows, our country, and mankind. We learn of the nine great Masonic Virtues that are built upon the three great pillars of Wisdom, strength, and beauty. They are truthfulness, endurance, independence, justice, mercy, equity, silence, devotion, and attainment. In this degree, we are given the key to self-knowledge and how we must learn to work for work's sake, for it shall make us better, and further do this without desire of praise or reward. This aspect tells us that it is our duty, as Masons, to seek and accumulate greater knowledge to know and practice ethical and moral principles that demonstrate man's highest, most noble nature. In the Degree of the Perfect Master (5th degree), we commemorate and recount the funereal ceremonies of our GMHA, and in doing so, it teaches the sobering lessons of death. We are taught to admonish death and how it may take us at any moment and realize that life is always fleeting; we must know that we do not have time to sit back and have it taken from us. It is our duty to our family and our loved ones to see that our affairs are in order and those whom we love and care about are well taken care of when we face the unimaginable departing of this life.

In the 6th Degree – Confidential Secretary, we discover Solomon and Hiram of Tyre in a private discussion. In the course of this discussion, Solomon's friend Zabud is thought to be eavesdropping and is threatened with punishment. With that drama unfolded, we are taught the excellence of disinterestedness and generosity; that is the duty of every true Mason to heal dissensions and differences and to further restore peace, concord, and harmony amongst men. Further, we are taught the necessity of good faith, fidelity, self-sacrifice, and generosity. Concepts such as self-control, of never rushing to judgment, and the nature of true friendship are taught to us as well, with more teachings of how zeal for service is always encouraged. And in the 7th degree – Provost and Judge, we learn of King Solomon and how it is enduring construction. This teaches us to be just, without which no man is fit to be free. The central idea states that above all else, Reverence and Administration of the Law is to be done with justice, equity, and impartiality. It teaches that it is an unjust man who assumes powers that are not his own, and that justice and uprightness alone can unlock the mysteries contained in higher degrees.

In the 8th degree, we learn that the inclination of knowledge without application leads to little or no value to us. We are taught about dignity and the importance of work, and those who perform it are the ones who are rewarded with advancement. We learn of the rights of the laboring classes and our duties toward them, but especially how impressive it is that every laboring man is our brother, entitled to our own regard and resistances.

In the 9th and 10th degrees, the Elu of the Nine and the Elu of the Fifteen, we are said to become pledged to the cause of true freedom, of the people, as distinguished from the mob and populace. We promise none should repent relying on our resolve, our word, and our profession. We are shown the virtues that should be displayed by one in the pursuit of justice: disinterestedness, courtesy, devotedness, firmness, frankness, generosity, self-denial, heroism, and loyalty. We are then exhorted to labor, to instruct, to inform, and to enlighten the people when called upon to do so, and to devote ourselves to the honor and interest of our country. We are focused toward the central idea that we should be reminded that everything that appears in these degrees is a symbol of something else, and we are called upon to reach beyond the surface of appearance and seek deeper meanings. Further, we swear an eternal vigilance against those special enemies of Freedom, which are said to be intolerance and persecution.

In the Elu of the Twelve, the 11th degree, we continue the tale of the 9th and 10th degrees. We are particularly reminded that revenge is ultimately met by the hand of god, though we must pursue evil to its deepest recesses of our efforts to defeat it. We are further taught to deal fairly with all men and see that none are subjected to extortion or the unjust imposition of burdens. Neither fear nor fault of our own may permit harm to fall upon our country or its people. We learn the value of trial by jury is extolled, without which liberty and immunity from wrong and oppression cannot be guaranteed. We are shown herein how an independent judiciary is the third leg upon which a stable and just government stands.

The 12th degree is filled with brief ceremonies and profound significance. Here, we are taught the symbolic meanings of the Master Architect's tools, the most important of which instructs us to solve the great problems presented by the universe, to know and understand the lofty truths of philosophy, and to communicate it freely to others, particularly by our actions. Only the best and wisest in us and among us should rule. For if it be any other, the low and the ignoble will presume and soon prevail.

The 13th degree, which goes together with the 14th, represents the capstone of the Lodge of Perfection and culminates with our descent on the floor of the ninth vault where we saw, without knowing it, the Lost Word. In this degree, we will witness a symbolic descent into the earth where the remains of a temple are discovered. The descent may represent many things. It may be emblematic of the difficulties encountered by those who endeavor to discover the truth about god and the world around us, often believing it may represent the self-exploration each of us must make in our quest for Truth. Nonetheless, the 14th degree is both a celebration of the revelation received in the 13th degree as well as an examination of our worthiness to possess it. We are taught that knowledge without its application is of little or no value. With knowledge comes responsibility, and one must prove oneself worthy to possess it. The mere possession of knowledge is not a virtue yet; knowledge properly applied results in wisdom, which the Book of Proverbs says was coexistent with creation. In this degree, we will be symbolically purified and consecrated to living virtuously, acting worthily, and deciding justly.

In the 15th degree, we learn of the ruins of the Temple of Perfection that we believe so secure in the previous degrees. It teaches us that it must be built again and that there is a great law of ebb and flow in Nature. We are forced to seek a solution in enigmas such as the confrontation with the reality of polarity, or opposition in all things. And, above all else, we are taught that we must remain faithful adherents to the Truth and practice correct behavior. Integrity is extolled as the rule and bylaw of our personal code. By the words "liberty of passage," we understand this as freedom of thought and conscience and political and religious liberty. Furthermore, the 16th degree continues the lessons of the 15th degree with an emphasis on the belief that God aids those who pursue a good work, are faithful, and can practice the virtue of Wisdom. We are taught that righteousness and the impartiality of Justice are again demonstrated to every Mason while being shown how difficult it is to rebuild the Temple of Liberty once it has been overthrown. We are taught the symbolic meaning of rebuilding the temple and the purposes of the Scottish Rite Masonry, religion founded on Love and Toleration, philosophy that springs from Faith in One God and Hope of a future life, morality that embodies the Wisdom of all ages, and a political creed that rests on three great pillars of Liberty, Equality, and Brotherhood.

The 17th Degree is split into two sections: The first being the confrontation between King Herod II and John the Baptist, which results in shameful murder of the latter, while the second section borrows symbolism from St. John's apocalyptic vision of the end of time. With this in mind, we are again commended to the virtues of Union, Honor, Duty, Loyalty, Courage, Discretion, and Silence. We are instructed that our lives must mirror our spirituality, and that knowledge of the name of God revealed to us in the 13th and 14th degrees must be applied knowledge. For once one realizes a truth, one must live in conformity with it. We are informed that innocence and Purity of Heart are prerequisites to the revelation of Great Mysteries, preparing you for the New Law in the 18th degree. We are informed that the path to wisdom, understanding, and knowledge we seek is not an easy one but perhaps fraught with pain, suffering, and great service. And finally, we cover the 18th degree, which places a focus on Honor. In this degree, we will be given the True Word and offered a solution to the great paradox of good and evil. We are taught to declare that we accept all good men of whatever creed and faith as our own brethren and understand that freemasonry may teach great truths that do not exclusively belong to any one particular religion. We are then taught to honor every reformer who has offered up his or her own life for the benefit of all humanity.

17

19th Degree
Grand Pontiff

I n the 19th Degree – the Grand Pontiff, the jewel is an oblong square of solid gold that contains two letters: Aleph and Tau, both being engraved on their gold squares. These letters are the first and last of the Hebrew alphabet, and those upon the cordon are of the Greek. These letters are intended to be placed openly to remind us of the love and veneration we owe to the one and only God, the source of all existence, the Alpha and Omega, the first and the last. On this, we know his promises that we rely on with perfect confidence, in whose mercy and goodness we implicitly trust, and nonetheless for the fulfillment of whose wise purposes we are content to wait. We must know that with all we must do with this world, our family, our nature, we must not use the limits of one life, for our plan as Masons surpass the time limit we have on our own lives. We must use the faith and do what we can to pass down for the benefit of others.

It is known that the true Mason labors for not only himself but for his loved ones and those who come after him. This is for a mere advancement of all our ideas and the utterly important True Word. With the idea of "the first and the last," it is vital for every Mason to remember that we have duties, virtues, and qualities that are seen vital under the 19th degree – the Grand Pontiff, which include being content to the labors of the future, serving the cause of truth with patience and industry, and to destroy error, falsehood, and intolerance with trust, honesty, honor, and charity. We are to remember that the human intellect cannot measure the designs of God, and we must have faith that if lived properly, this life is a bridge to eternal life.

The idea of the bridge is vital as well, for it contains the idea that we all serve a greater purpose. This is the idea of this degree; we must all work for the common good, that being, the bridge to eternal life. In addition, this notion is best phrased by "The Bridge Builder," written by William Charles Beller, which states:

"Pontifices the Romans named their priests: Bridge Builders; for they wrought a bridge 'twixt Gods and Mortals, framed of rite and legend, deed and thought. Bridge Builder in a later year Am I, who, seeking still the truth, with woven words essay to rear a bridge between the old and new. Far off, across the stream of time, The light of ancient Hellas gleams; And latter ages, less sublime, Are guided by those distant beams. Between, as black as midnight sea, Ages of darkness roll their tides. By that dim waste the light may be Obscured, but still the light abides. The light that shone in ancient Greece Shall in our times once more arise, And match the younger years' increase With vaster worlds in vaster skies. I do but strive, in night and storm, to stretch a slender span alight. Let those affirmer fabric forms Who labor in the morning light! For still the wildered wanderer needs to reach the light that shines afar, Where, through the storm of warring creeds, Truth gleamed as a guiding star."

This idea is the encompassing idea of the 19th degree, the hope that the pursuit of the first and the last is what embodies the trust and love in belief we must obtain in our education and thus, the source of our existence—the greater good.

In Pike's *Morals and Dogma*, he discusses the tide of human endeavor and that we come together as a unit. He claims that all human thought, speech, and action is all done and said to ponder and suffer upon the earth in order to combine together and flow onward in a metaphor of a flowing river, as a single impenetrable unit. He says we must flow onward in one broad resistless current toward those great results, that being God's plan, to which they are determined by the will of God. We are known to build slowly and destroy swiftly, so with this we must remember that everything takes time, and we must remember the vital morals we are taught in not only this degree but every degree. Slow but steady wins the race; we must be patient and remember our true wants and needs, the success of life, and love within our beliefs. It is well-known that our ancient brothers who built the temples of Jerusalem with primitive methods that took a lot of time acted in such a way we can look up to for centuries to come. But nonetheless, with the combined efforts of our past brethren as well as the long toil of apprenticeship, fellow-craft, and master, the wall arose; slowly the roof was framed and fashioned, and many years elapsed before, at length, the houses stood finished, all fit and ready for the worship of God. This was considered as more than simply a glorious obstacle, but more as a single notion that incorporated the splendors of the best atmosphere, and that being a standard to set is saying a ton.

According to the 19th degree – Grand Pontiff, we notice that there are ways to improve the world (for lack of a better phrase), and by considering the enormity of the positions we hold, we can be used to make the world a better place. Through these virtues we are taught how we can help, through the sense of our individual efforts in which we have enough power and goodness to help those in life, especially those who come after us. These virtues are incorporated through many of the ideas described in Pike's *Morals and Dogma*. In *Morals and Dogma* under the 19th degree and the Grand Pontiff, we immediately see that it is in the duty of every mason to labor for the benefit for those who come after us, and us being Masons can use our efforts in order to help others advance and improve race, specifically speaking of one's own race. Pike remarks how all men who deserve to live and desire to survive their funerals and even those who live afterward in the good that mankind has bettered should do so instead of becoming fading characters written in a man's memories. Pike made it clear that every man's soul is just as important as its living one, and thus, we should know that as men, as Masons, we should not desire to leave any work behind.

We should be able to leave this world knowing that what we have set to conquer has been completed thoroughly. In the case where this hasn't or will not be done, Pike remarks how these efforts laid aside and uncompleted may outlast their own day and brief generation, meaning that they will still haunt us, for a job left undone is something that should not be done. Furthermore, it is an instinctive impulse given by God and often found in the rudest hearts. This entire idea is about leaving the world behind better than the way we came in. We should always strive to better something, whether it's a life or a family or a way of being. We should always know, as Masons, and as men, that it is our obligation to finish our moral duties honorably, leaving no slack behind for others to pick up, for this idea of making the world better comes with the departing of one whose efforts of completing his life goals should be noticed and leakcd into other lives as something other than work left behind. These efforts are meant to be there as a support, a way of letting us know that by leaving goodness for those after us, we are, in a huge way, helping many others after us.

Through our efforts, we are in fact helping many others and thus doubting our efforts. Pike explains this analogy, which describes how our virtues are symbolically paid off later in life and after life: The idea of the Grand Pontiff is to plant the trees that, after we are dead, shall shelter our children, is as natural as to love the shade of those our fathers planted to provide for us. It's a universal cycle that we learn as Masons, as men, which will better the lives after us.

The very fabrication of why we learn in specific ways comes into question with the idea of "the first and the last." It has conceptual meaning very similar to the ways in which we learn about the degrees. Conceptually, the degrees are considered the many steps of the mystic ladder, by which we pass down and incorporate into our everyday lives the knowledge of the True Word, to the knowledge of God and of Nature, which all Masons should know is vital for His Revelation. According to *The Scottish Rite Monitor and Guide*, the degrees are therefore considered instructions by symbols and their interpretations in political, philosophical, and religious knowledge. If they are unable to be seen as such, they are nothing or merely vain and empty ceremonies that can never be seen as useless or unable to pass on the True Word. Masonry must teach the truth or die; that's its main objective. It lives only by teaching the truth, by one soul at a time, and encouraging them to pass it on as a chain reaction, to start at the beginning then going to the end. Furthermore, God, being infinite, is known by us only by His finite manifestations; the known leading us, by necessary or reasonable hypothesis, to the divine, a relative unknown, and the wisdom of God, by which everything begins and ends—the principle of all that eternally exists. This consists in the spirit of loving-kindness or charity. It created the universe, and it preserves it, and its dissolution is regeneration. To it alone the soul owes its immortality; and whatsoever, in Masonry or in political conduct or in religion, is contrary to this spirit and this Supreme Wisdom is false.

18

20th Degree
Master of the Symbolic Lodge

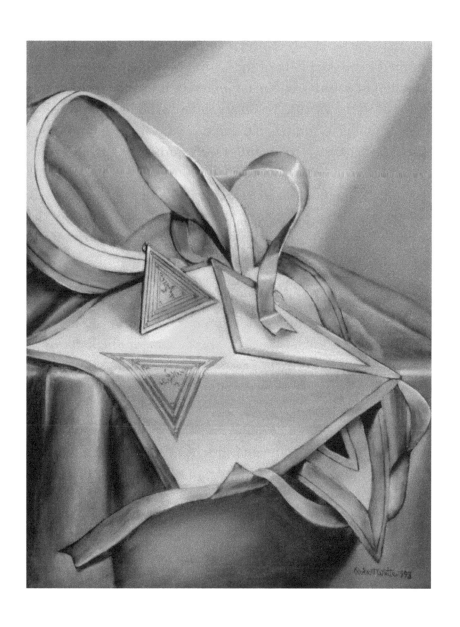

The fundamental obligation of a Lodge Master is fulfilled by the True Mason, and this obligation can be filled by the actions taken by that Mason. For a Lodge Master, it is his obligation to be a true Mason, and by that, I mean the very truthful and morally correct words of Albert Pike. It is said that he must be a practical philosopher, one who, under religious emblems, in all ages are adopted by wisdom. This is vital for it is the wisdom of the Lodge Master to build upon that and plan a trace by nature and reason for the moral edifice of knowledge; it is the principle and rule of all his duties and the source of all his pleasures. He improves his moral nature, becomes a better man, and finds in the reunion of virtuous men, assembled with pure views, the means of multiplying his acts of beneficence (ideas taught to us through the study of the degrees). Masonry and Philosophy, without being one and the same thing, have the same object, and propose to themselves the same end, the worship of the Grand Architect of the Universe, acquaintance and familiarity with the wonders of nature, and the happiness of humanity attained by the constant practice of all the virtues. These are described best by Pike, who remarks the countless number of duties that are required for the honorable title of Grand Master. Yet, although these duties seem endless, it is in the responsibility of the Lodge Master to ensure the continuance of these ideas and teach them to others, for this is the best way to strive for the bettering of a future.

Furthermore, as Grand Master of all symbolic lodges, it is especially their duty to aid the efforts of restoring Masonry to its primitive purity. It is said that you would have to become an instructor, even though Masonry has long wandered in error; it is this that the Lodge Master would designate that instead of improving, it degenerated from its primitive simplicity, and retrograded toward a system, distorted by stupidity and ignorance, which we should avoid. This idea comes from the fact that we should act the same in the lodge as we would outside the lodge, for this is part of the system of teachings; it is never-ending and should never end. These ideas should always continue, for they have been known to end in the past. But it was in the past where its organization was simple, and altogether moral; its emblems, allegories, and ceremonies easy to be understood, and their purpose and idea of objects readily seen. It was then confined to a very small number of degrees in which constitutions were similar to those of a Society of Essence. And so, the ideas of this degree are incorporated with the idea to fraternize with all men, assist all those who are unfortunate, cheerfully postpone their own interests to that of the order. And furthermore, to make it the constant rule of their lives to think well, to speak well, and to act well. This would be understood as a way for the obligations of the Lodge Master to be successfully fulfilled.

In the *Scottish Rite Ritual Monitor and Guide*, the synopsis remarks: "Truth, Justice, toleration as the rule of life, conduct, and conversation," and if one were to think about this in terms of the main objective of a Grand Master, this is a perfect shortened phrase that sums it all up. Pioneers like Pike would take a statement like this as far as humanly possible, for it stands as a totem pole to which the Grand Master should not only abide by but should actively pursue in the oncoming years. It's vital.

One of the major ideas this chapter portrays as a vital aspect of becoming and being the Grand Master is this: It is not only what one must and should do throughout their life, but it also acts upon a vital idea of what you leave behind, just as we discussed with past degrees on leaving a well-benefited family long after we go. On this topic, Pike remarks: "The true Mason labors for the benefit of those who are to come after him and for the advancement and improvement of his race." There is a huge notion that we must leave the world better than how we received it, for anything other than that is a poor ambition which contents itself within the limits of a single life. This idea goes beyond our own life expectancy; it bleeds into future generations. This also regards men who believe they deserve to live, who have the desire to survive their funerals and to live afterward in the good that they have done for mankind rather than in the fading characters written in man's memories.

By this notion, Pike remarks that we may or may not be remembered going through life doing the best we can, but by acting in these manners, we can ensure that men who follow our life, and who carry out the good word and continue to pursue the Grand Master, must realize that it may take many generations to accomplish. Slow but steady wins the race: This concept lies in the notion that we must slowly do our part and pave the way for future generations to help us finish the task at hand. Furthermore, it can be understood that most men desire to leave some work behind them that may outlast their own day and brief generation; that is an instinctive impulse, given by God, and often found in the rudest human heart; the surest proof of the soul's immortality and of the fundamental difference between man and the wisest brutes.

One idea that will forever stick with me is the metaphor described in Pike's *Morals and Dogma*, in which he explains that in order to plan the trees that, after we are dead, shall shelter our children, is as natural as to love the shade of those our fathers planted. The rudest unlettered husbandman, painfully conscious of his own inferiority, the poorest widowed mother, given her life-blood to those who pay only for the work of her needle, will toil and stint themselves to educate their child, that he may take a higher station in the world than they; and of such are the world's greatest benefactors.

Just as the importance of when a man is to die, he must ensure that his family will be well off, how much better would it be for that family's survival if everything they will ever need to know can be taught by previous generations? This notion states that by learning from our elders we can gain the help needed. This is the vital point: We cannot have a successful pursuit of life without some form of help, and who better to give us that help than our own family and common brothers? In addition, in *A Bridge to Light*, it is understood that it is the dead that govern, and the living only obey. They should see that after death, the importance lies on what passes on the earth and watch over the welfare of those they love. Then must their greatest happiness consist in seeing the current of their beneficent influences widening out from age to age. For a Grand Master, this is the act of aiding to shape the destinies of people, families, states, and the world in contrast to the bitterest punishment, in seeing its evil influences causing mischief and misery, and cursing and afflicting men, long after the frame it has been dealt—this is when the good, long-lasting memory can be forgotten.

Thus, The Lodge Master as well as all living humans must obey the dead, similarly to when we are dead, for weal or woe, the living should obey us. The thoughts of the past are the laws of the present and the future. In sum, that which we say and do, if the effects of that do not last beyond our lives, it is unimportant. That we shall live when we are dead, as part of the great body of law enacted by the dead, is the only act worth doing, the only thought worth speaking. The desire to do something that shall benefit the world, when neither praise nor obloquy will reach us where we sleep soundly in the grave, is the noblest ambition entertained by man. It is that very ambition of a true and genuine Mason. Knowing the slow processes by which the Deity brings about great results, he does not expect to reap as well as sow in a single lifetime. The long-lasting fate that is the inevitable though noblest destiny, with rare expectations, of the great and good, is to work and let others reap the harvest of their labors. He who does good only to be repaid in kind, or in thanks and gratitude, or in reputation and the world's praise, is like him who loans money and knows that in time he shall trustingly receive it back with interest, for it shall be fair and what is entrusted to him.

In closing, it's important to ensure that Masons and men alike are not to be faint. Never be nor become faint, for you shall never be weary in well-doing.

A Master in general is to be not discouraged at man's apathy, nor disgusted with their follies, nor tired of their indifference—never care for returns and results but see only what there is to do, and by doing it, you will leave promising results to God, the Soldier of the Cross, Sworn Knight of Justice, truth and toleration—remembering that a Good Knight, especially a Lodge Master, must be true to being patient and working.

19

According to *A Bridge to Light*, the 21st degree or Noachite (Prussian Knight) is conducted very similarly to many of the other degrees yet is differentiated in many ways. To this degree, the most important duties of every Mason is to be humble and modest, trusting in God as well as being steadfast and courageous in the face of adversity. This is a major vital embodiment that one must possess in order to follow the ideals of this degree. The lessons are meant to teach us that the downfall of evil is certain, and this tells us to hold our heads up high and fight for the greater future. In the realm of all this lies the center foundation of this degree, Albert Pike. He is most commonly known for his writings in *Morals and Dogma* in which he discusses the ideals of the degrees one by one just as *A Bridge to Light* does, except it's filled with an opinion filled by a brother who is quite often seen as a figure of great pursuit. In this essay, I set forth to accomplish the further understanding of Pike's remarks in *Morals and Dogma* in which the above stated comes with the understanding that every Mason must portray.

In the discussion of this degree, Pike begins by saying, "You are especially charged in this Degree to be modest and humble, and neither vain-glorious nor filled with self-conceit." This is meant to tell Masonry as a whole to understand that the best of notions has been laid out by the Deity, and it's not in our best interest to be wiser than it. As well, the 4th degree states that it is vital to embody humility and modesty as virtues not for the reason of learning, but rather, the effect is for the best interest of men as a whole. He continues by ensuring these notions with the hope that fellow Masons do not find fault in God's works nor endeavor to improve what God has done. This tells us to be modest in our life course with others and our fellow man, to be slow to entertain evil thoughts, and to further be reluctant to ascribe to them evil intentions. This notion comes with the belief that if you truly aspire to be a true Mason, following the Deity is the only path necessary. Having this idea in our everyday life can never be a bad thing, and by this, we are given the tools to be successful in life. This is how this passage as well as the 4th and 21st degree are shown to embody men who are able to function in everyday life and become successors. Learning to be modest and humble toward life and being successful are the tools given in this degree that can ensure a healthy, happy, and proper fulfillment in life. This comes down to jobs, relationships, and our personal morals, all of which are vital when we portray who we are to a job executive, for example. This can even be taken as far as teaching to our children.

In an overarching notion, this degree sets out to teach every Mason that advocating the acts of being humble and modest are what we are charged with to show how glorious we can be. Because of this, Pike tells every Mason that we all, commonly, can achieve greatness. But he makes it clear multiple times that evil is always around and will always be there. The bad temptations and things we should endure are not necessary, and by following these ideas and notions provided by Pike, one can ensure happiness overall. If every Mason, and better yet, every man embodies this, we may be given a chance to pursue world peace. Now, one may think that world peace is impossible, but Pike believes it's simply a conflict of notions. Pike continues to say that evil is widespread and universal and that no man, woman, or household is safe or sacred from the inquisition that evil places on the world. World peace will never be an easy thing for humans or mankind to accomplish, but that doesn't mean we should ever stop the pursuit. This is the point of this degree, to be honest and modest of our current state and want change through determinism and diligence. We should believe that we can accomplish anything. Let it be known that it is the duty of every Mason to act pure and praiseworthy, that the unscrupulous vender of lies who lives by pandering to a corrupt or morbid public appetite will not proclaim it as a crime. No motive is so innocent or so laudable that he will not hold up as villainy. Pike is very aware of the evils presented in many aspects in life and in the idea of world peace. Even the connection of bettering relationships is no easy task, for even with the building of relationships, evil is presented and will always be. This should never stop any Mason, for we know that evil is enlarged in many aspects in life, and with every breath it diverges us from what we are meant to do in life, which is to believe in the Deity with respect and power, believing in being virtuous.

Given in this degree are many tools, and whether we realize them and take them in our own hands to pursue is on us. Pike makes it clear that no one will help us in the pursuit of life as a whole, this along with the little counterparts that bombastically fill life. There is no obligation resting on us to trumpet forth the disapproval of every wrongful or injudicious or improper act that every other man commits. We must weigh the bad and good, and take both for as they are, but the most important part lies in the ACT. The act is the embodiment that Pike and Masons commonly try to follow.

Furthermore, a generality given by Pike has caught my attention that addresses how one might display how various acts can be interpreted and be taken as they are for the notions that lie with them. In this, Pike explains that the censure bestowed upon a man's acts, by those very men who have appointed and commissioned themselves keepers of the public morals, is undeserved. Often it is not only undeserved, but praise is undeserved instead of censure, and, when the latter is not undeserved, it is always extravagant, and therefore unjust. These various unjust acts lie with our pursuit of justice. This is something we must always keep a grasp on, for it is the responsibility and duty of every Mason to be fruitful in the protection of justice, not to be interpreted as taking the law into one's own hands, but simply stating to be careful, fruitful, and gracefully protect them. Our acts are a big part of this degree to which a man can place one's self in the position he pleases when it comes down to relationships and in the business realm. Pike states that arrogance is a big part of the acts that men portray, for it is the very weak that ever grows on a dunghill. It is from the rankness of that soil that she hath her height and spreading, for it can be contagious.

Nevertheless, there is but one rule for the Mason in the matter of embodiment of the previously mentioned virtues. If there be virtues, and he is called up to speak of him to who owns the thoughts, that being every Mason, it should be told to them impartially. If there are vices mixed with them, let him be content that the world shall know them by some other tongue than his. God is not one who sulks, and if there is an evil-doer, you must be aware of such acts of evil and react appropriately. Finally, Pike remarks, "the Mason should be humble and modest toward the Grand Architect of the Universe." This sets out to tell every Mason not to impugn his wisdom nor set up his own imperfect sense of right against his providence and dispensations, nor attempt to rashly to explore the mysteries of God's infinite essence and instructable plans and of that great nature that we are not capable to understand. We are given these tools with the hopes that we actively follow them; this is the hope of fellow Masons as well as Albert Pike. With the tools given and the guidance of God, we are to follow these various notions in order to successfully build on relationships and to ensure the best chance and way of living for every man, not just Masons.

Furthermore, when a Mason hears of any man that has fallen in a public view, he should have a mind to commiserate his mishap and not to make him more disconsolate. To envenom a name by libels that already is openly tainted is to add stripes with an iron rod to one who is flayed with whipping, and to every well-tempered will seems most inhuman and unmanly . With all that has been stated in mind, Pike shows every Mason that the way we carry ourselves is the key to being a successful Mason as well as being successful in the pursuit of bettering relationships and our dire need to be more business-savvy. In closing, none of what I said will it be easy, but evermore, standing humbly and reverently upon the earth and looking with awe and confidence toward Heaven, let him be satisfied that there is a real God: a person, and not a formula: a Father and a protector, who loves, and sympathizes, and is compassionate; and that the eternal ways by which God rules the world are the ways of the infinitely wise, no matter how far they may be above the feeble comprehension and limited vision of Man.

20

22nd Degree
Knight Royal Axe, or Prince of Libanus

In *Morals and Dogma*, we are taught that work is the mission of a man. This should never be confused with a curse, but should be thought of more so as the fulfillment of life's purpose. Our daily labor, if fit and proper, receives the blessing of God. If the employer understands the dignity even of simple labor, then the employee will not be oppressed. Personally, I believe that with the virtues of work comes pay-offs that can benefit us more than what is seen with the naked eye. As Masons, we are taught that all work is noble and sacred that is derived from virtue, something taught to us through past degrees. But from this degree, the 22nd, we must have respect for the labor itself, and with sympathy, we must resolve to do some good work in our day and generation. These ideas are the basis of the idea of labor, and thus derived from a purely Masonic standpoint.

Masonry can make the working man and his associates the heroes of her principal legend, and as Pike remarks, himself the companion of Kings. The idea is as simple and true as it is sublime. From first to last, Masonry is work. And labor is life. It venerates the Grand Architect of the Universe. It commemorates the building of a Temple. Its principal emblems are the working fools of Masons and Artisans. It preserves the name of the first worker in brass and iron as one of its passwords. Even when the Brethren meet together, they are at labor. The Master is the overseer who sets the craft to work and gives them proper instruction. Masonry is the apotheosis of work. It is the hands of brave, forgotten men that have made this great, populous, cultivated world a world for us. It is all work, and forgotten work. These are the ideas of this degree, which fulfill the notion that every Mason is a hard worker, and because of that comes the appreciation of the work itself, for it can teach us far more than simply working toward a goal and the common well-being of every human being. Furthermore, we must understand that a man's highest destiny is to be happy, to love pleasant things and find them. His only true unhappiness should be that he cannot work and get his destiny as a man fulfilled. And as the days pass, he should only remember how he can be happy, and through his work, he can begin to incorporate happiness in his life, for it is his destiny. Duty is with us forever and evermore forbids us to be idle. To work with the hands or brain, and according to our requirements and our capacities, as men, fathers, brothers, husbands, and Masons, to do that which lies before us to do, is more honorable than rank and title. Pike notes in *Morals and Dogma* that ploughers, spinners, and builders, inventors, and men of science, poets, advocates, and writers, all stand upon one common level and form one grand, innumerable host, marching ever onward since the beginning of the world; each entitled to our sympathy and respect, each a man and our brother.

This is what is meant by "labor is work." It's the idea that no matter what a man does, it does not entail his qualifications in life, but rather, how one conducts themselves during the time in which they work is more important. It is vital for every man and Mason alike to understand, cope, and strive for these virtues. As our readings tell us, respect is in the labor itself. They are the same virtues we set out to teach our young ones. In that, we claim that it's not the work itself, but it's the embodiment one puts into the virtues of work. For doing such honest, moral, and just activities, we are able to show that we can labor for what we want. These virtues do not set us out to be part of a working class but to have class in itself. With the class of such virtues, we can come raise our young boys into men. These are not only the duties of Masons, but for men in general.

With this in mind, it was the mindful words of Albert Pike, yet again, who can never put any of these ideals into such better words as these: "Whatsoever of morality and intelligence: What of patience, perseverance, faithfulness, of method, insight, ingenuity, energy; in a word, Whatsoever of STRENGTH a man has in him, will lie written in the work he does." Now, my attempt to derive such awe-inspiring words took me quite a while. Here's what I came up with. A man, any man, all men, must act and support the activities one pursues. He cannot just strive for work simply because of the initial benefits that come from it; money, free time, helping out. Though those are good bonuses for such deep virtues, the real meaning of these acts lies in the aftermath of doing them. The importance in work and more so, the pay-off from laboring shall not be immediately shown. They must take time to settle, and after the exhaustion of laboring, one will then, and only then, see the aftermath of virtues. Furthermore, for a man to embody patience and perseverance is arguably the hardest thing to do. I have had plenty of experience with family members or friends claiming that "it's too hard," or that "things are easier to quit." And to be frank, all it takes is some inspiration. So I quote Pike, and just hearing what it takes is inspirational. Even talking to my friends and family, to be there for them, to help and support them, is work and labor in my life. These are things I have to show faith in; I must be energetic, and I must have strength. For this is the only way we can grow. At least for me, this is my personal interpretation of labor being work. Everything in life, one way or another, contains a form of work, a form of labor. And to achieve anything in life, one must act as every Mason set out to act.

This also entails the idea that one must be heroic. You cannot give up due to hardships, for life will always and forever test you. Test your will, test your character. If life was easy, everyone would be successful, powerful, and endless in acquired desires. But life is not like this. Life is relentless, so it is utterly important to remember that we can achieve anything through work and labor. We must grow and adapt to all things big and small. To work and labor for life means to endorse well-being. If you think about it, our human existence is fulfilled with endless examples of laboring over work, and how this work can pay off. The historical continuum of our lives will exemplify and reflect what we have done in our lives through work. This is our duty as Masons; as is the oldest of times, this will never change. Through all the trials and tribulations, through all the chaos, and through all the internal and external attacks, we must work. And by doing so, we must embody the idea that labor is life.

On the other hand, it is equally as important that we must know and recognize that evils are present. It's hard to swallow, but we must all be reminded of it. It is lurking, constantly around us and attempting to clinch its grasp on those who are weak. Masonry teaches us to keep our faith in God. He is our commander, and we must attack all ignorance, stupidity, and brute-mindedness, whether it comes to our faiths or virtues. This alone is work, keeping one's faith in God. This belief runs along with the idea that we must never rest while we live. Without these virtues, there could be no true excellence in human nature. As Pike remarks in *Morals and Dogma*, "without it, and pain, and sorrow, where would be the human virtues? Where patience, perseverance, submission, energy, endurance, fortitude, bravery, disinterestedness, self-sacrifice, the noblest excellencies of the soul." Furthermore, we are taught in this degree that we must not complain, nor feel humiliated. Duty will forever stick with us, and for evermore forbid us to relax and keep calm. This is a requirement. To substantiate an honorable man, filled with rank and title, to ensure our family's health, care, and well-being lies in what we do. And what we do is labor. For labor is life.

In closing, Masonry teaches us that every person must endure some field of labor. That's the only way to "get anywhere" in life. Either mental or manual, spiritual or physical, psychological or physiological, we must never convert to one who does not labor. This is a sin, or can be interpreted as a sin, as a way of giving up and throwing in the towel, so to speak. We must improve, get better, and strive for more. Our lives are relentless, and I believe that the ultimate belief and notion of this degree lies in the virtues of work, despite our imperfect civilization. Nothing is perfect, and nor can we ever be perfect. But perfection is never tested by doing something to a tee, more so, it's a testament of time, work, dignity, and honor, which all ensure a discipline that we all, including myself, must act upon. Ultimately, I would like to close with the wise words of none other than Albert Pike: "The great law of human industry is this: That industry, working either with the hand or the mind, the application of our powers to some task, to the achievement of some result, lies at the foundation of all human improvement. We are not sent into the world like animals, to crop the spontaneous herbage of the field, and then to lie down in indolent repose: but we are sent to dig the soul and plough the sea; to do the business of cities and the world of manufactories. The world is the great and appointed school of industry.... Labor is man's great function, his peculiar distinction and his privilege."

21

23rd Degree
Chief of the Tabernacle

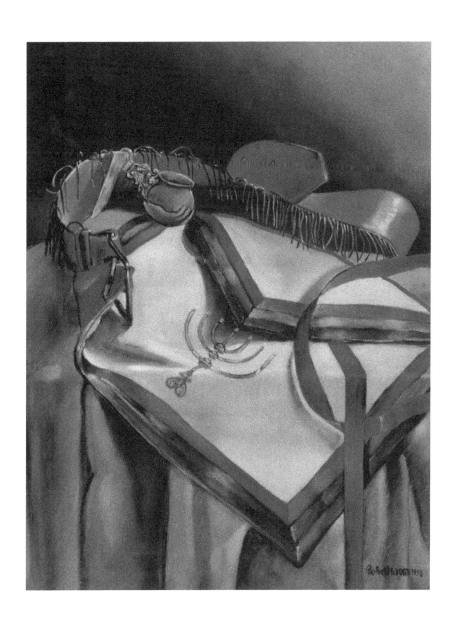

T he 23rd degree begins the symbolic initiation into the mysteries practiced by the ancients from whom Masonry has obtained their great truths. The duties of this degree state that simple faith is wider than mere philosophy, and by this, Masonry means that the concept of duty and the universe are consistent with development. We must set ourselves to think of the nature of God to which the moral lesson that portrays that devotion to the service of God; disinterested zeal and the bettering for the welfare of men are the characteristics of the lesser mysteries. As Albert Pike tells us, the use of symbols is the key concept. We are not meant to be simply told what something means; by this, Masonry remains in the shadows, as esoteric as possible to convey the secrecy and importance of private duty. Throughout one's study of this degree, one must realize that this degree lectures on the introduction and justification of the Mystery Degrees: Chief of the Tabernacle, Prince of the Tabernacle, Knight of the Brazen Serpent, and Prince of Mercy—these varied mysteries had common purposes and treatment of God, Man, and Nature.

While the tenets in question were for the purpose of learning the lesser mysteries, we are informed about the Greater Mysteries, despite having the "true spirit and secret doctrine hidden," stating the importance of ritualistic secrecy and initiation. Plato said that "the object of the Mysteries was to re-establish the soul in its primitive purity and in that state of perfection which it had lost," thus showing that it is instituted by our Masters, for the instruction of man and the correction of morals is key. Winding down to the focus on esoteric knowledge, we must know as Masons that the processes of initiations are to elevate the soul from a material, sensual, and purely human life to a communion and celestial intercourse with the Gods; this is key. There is a variety of forms this can be done in, for the purity of morals and elevation of the soul were required to the initiates. Now, people can just read these various notions and try to understand the meaning, but as seen through our historical continuum, the various instructions and meanings of degrees were done by symbols. This is an important concept when considering the esoteric learning curve for this type of knowledge.

Plato said that the object of the Mysteries was to re-establish the soul in its primitive purity and in that state of perfection that it had lost. The point of esoteric knowledge is to not be told something, but to learn it vicariously through our studies of Masonic theory. This is vital and is often done through rituals and initiations. The purpose of initiations is to elevate the soul from a material, sensual, and purely human life to a communion and celestial intercourse with the gods. And, a variety of things, forms, and species were shown initiates, representing the first generations of the gods. In symbolic forms of the mysteries exhibited the ONE, of which the manifold is an infinite illustration, containing a moral lesson, calculated to guide the soul through life and to cheer it in death. It must be known, as Masons, that the spiritual regeneration of man was typified in the Mysteries by the second birth of Dionysus as offspring of the highest, and the agents and symbols of that regeneration were the elements that affected Nature's periodical purification—the air, indicated by the mystic fan, the fire, signified by the torch, and the baptismal water, for water is not only cleanser of all things, but the genesis or source of all. This is most commonly seen and yet, little understood, about baptisms. They are ritualistic notions that hold esoteric meanings and religious purposes that people hold true to their beliefs. So why do so? The answer lies in the meaning behind such initiations. This is the purpose of this degree.

As Pike best describes: Those notions, clothed in ritual, suggested the souls, reformation and training, the moral purity formally proclaimed at Eleusis. He only was invited to approach, which was 'of clean hands and ingenuous speech, free from all pollution, and with a clear conscience.' 'Happy the man,' say the initiated in Euripides and Aristophanes, 'who purifies his life, and who reverently consecrates his soul in the thirsts of the God.'" It is claimed by Pike that "they whom Proserpine guides in her mysteries," it was said, "who imbibed her instruction and spiritual nourishment, rest from their labors and know strife no more." One must be happy they are to witness and comprehend these sacred ceremonies. They are made to know the meaning of the riddle of existence by observing its aim and termination as appointed by Zeus; they partake a benefit more valuable and enduring than the grain bestowed by wares, for they exalted their mental capacity in obtaining sweet desires and hopes. As Masons, there is no doubt that the ceremonies of initiation were originally few and simple. The great truths of the primitive revelation faded out of the memories of the masses of the people. This barely touches the surface of what is meant by esoteric knowledge.

In this degree we learn that, in fact, Ancient Greece isn't the only society that became accustomed to purification by water. Water is seen as a basis to show many things, symbolically, and through its rituals it puts the meanings in terms of the active life. In many religions, these aims of rituals are to remove specifically defined uncleanliness prior to a particular type of activity, thus the use of water as a form of purification. For example, the Hebrew Bible has many rituals of purification relating to menstruation, childbirth, sexual relations, Keri (nocturnal emission), unusual bodily fluids, skin disease, death, and animal sacrifices. Baptism is a form of ritual purification that occurs in several religions related to Judaism and most prominently in Christianity. Christianity also has other forms of ritual purification. In older churches and modern Roman Catholic churches, there are a number of levers around the building for the laity to use as ritual symbolism of cleansing themselves, usually by dipping the fingertips in the holy water and then making the sign of the cross. In traditional liturgical churches, a laver, often embedded in the wall, exists for the priest and deacon to wash their hands before celebrating the Eucharist. Many ancient churches were built with a large fountain in the courtyard. It was the tradition for Christians to wash before entering the church for worship. This usage is also legislated in the Rule of St. Benedict, as a result of which, many medieval monasteries were built with communal lavers for the monks or nuns to wash up before the Daily Office.

Despite what is depicted later, especially by Christian writers who draw of the Mysteries, they must not only originally have continued the pure doctrines of what the natural religion and morals rituals teach—they have been of the highest importance because both the most virtuous as well as the most learned and philosophic of the ancients speak of them in the loftiest terms. Further, the rites of initiation became progressively more complicated. Signs and tokens were invented by which the Children of Light could know for the purpose of knowledge, hence why the degrees were invented. Originally, the mysteries were meant to be the beginning of a new life of reason and virtue. The initiated or esoteric companions were taught for the reason of understanding the One Supreme God, the theory of death and eternity, the hidden mysteries of nature, the prospect of the ultimate restoration of the soul to that state of perfection from which has been lost over time, and the states of reward and punishment after death. By initiations, those members are saved to which the uninitiated were deemed profane, unworthy of public employment or private confidence, sometimes prescribed as Atheists, and certain of everlasting punishment beyond the grave.

Pike best describes the importance of Greater Mysteries by claiming that "All persons were initiated into the lesser Mysteries; but few attained the greater, in which the true spirit of them, and most of their secret doctrines were hidden. The veil of secrecy was impenetrable, sealed by oaths and penalties the most tremendous and appalling. It was by initiation only, that a knowledge of the Hieroglyphics could be obtained, with which the walls, columns, and ceilings of the Temples were decorated, and which, believed to have been communicated to the Priests by revelation from the celestial deities, the youth of all ranks were laudable ambitious of deciphering."

On the other hand, Pythagoras taught in his lectures a medium that set out to prove the existence of God from observation and by means of reasons. This was done by grammar, rhetoric, and logic, to cultivate and improve that reason and arithmetic because he conceived that the better of a man was hidden in his knowledge in the science of numbers, geometry, music, and astronomy, because he conceived that man was indebted to them for a knowledge of what is really good and useful. We, as just other initiates, were taught the true method of obtaining knowledge of the Divine laws of purifying the soul from its imperfections. This is done by searching for truths and by practicing virtues thus imitating the perfections of God. This is the point of such secrecy. He thought his system vain if it did not contribute to expel vice and introduce virtue into the mind; he taught that the two most excellent things were to be honest by speaking the truth and to render benefits to all and one another. Keeping near to this notion are the following: in calculating silence, temperance, fortitude, prudence, and justice. We must learn to know, as Masons, that we must be taught the immortality of the soul, the omnipotence of God, and the necessity of personal holiness to qualify a man for admission into the society of the gods. Pike agrees with this notion, seen in his excerpt in *Morals and Dogma* in which he claims, "Thus we owe the particular mode of instruction in the Degree of Fellow-Craft to Pythagoras; and that Degree is but an imperfect reproduction of his lectures. From him, too, we have many of our explanations of the symbols."

Just as the early Christians, who were taught by their founder of their religion in "greater perfection" and were taught primitive truths from the latter by the Essences received also the institution of the Mysteries, they adopted it as their object of building the symbolic temple. As such, the doctrine of the Mysteries or that of the Tabernacle, to which we should all learn to admit, is the admission of the moral lesson of this degree, which is devotion to the service of God and disinterested zeal and constant endeavor for the welfare of men. Ultimately, we have received only hints of the true objects and purposes of the Mysteries, and if you are permitted to advance, you, my brother, as a Mason, will arrive at a more complete understanding of them and of the sublime doctrines that they teach. Be content, therefore, with that which you have seen and heard, and await patiently the advent of greater light. For it is all in due time.

22

24th Degree
Prince of the Tabernacle

Traditionally, faith and reason have been considered to be two of the sources of justification for religious and moral beliefs. Because both can purportedly serve the same function, it's been an interest of many focus groups and thus how this rational agent should treat claims derived from either source. This is tested, derived, and explained through the act of initiation. *A Bridge to Light* explains that the candidate is tested in his ability to process the human qualities that allow him to become a functional member of this brotherhood, so it is vital as Masons that we keep in mind that faith and reason play a vital part in many aspects of the degrees, especially this one, the 24th – Prince of the Tabernacle.

Firstly, there is the concept of symbols, which were almost the universal language of ancient theology. They were the way people instructed others. The first teachers of mankind barred various methods of instruction and consisted of tempting curiosity. The main focus is the concept of the Mysteries. This is the point of it all. The Ancient Sages, both barbarian and Greek, involved some form of indirection and enigmas, for their lessons were conveyed either in visible symbols or were considered sacred. The point of initiation is to focus on the capabilities of the person and portray the very detailed aspects of the fraternity. All the philosophers and legislators of the time who made initiations part of everyday life describe them as the beneficent modifications in the religions. The different people instructed by them were owing to their institution and extension of the Mysteries.

The idea lies, as it always shall, as a double object. As Pike describes, political and religious—one teaching our duty to men and the other what we owe to the gods, or rather, respect for the gods calculated to maintain that which we owe the laws. This is found in that well-known verse of Virgil, borrowed by him from the ceremonies of initiation. The point was to "teach one to respect justice and the gods." This is the great lesson that the hierophant impressed on the initiates after they had witnessed a representation of the Infernal regions the poet places after his description of the different punishments suffered by the wicket and immediately after the description of Sisyphus. During this process, aided by all the resources of art, is the virtuous man's happy life after death and the horrors of the frightful prisons destined to punish the vicious. For Masons, it is in the shades of these sanctuaries that these delights and horrors were exhibited as spectacles, and the initiates witnessed religious dramas under the name of initiation and the mysteries. This was the point of learning the mysteries of the fraternity; it was meant to teach us various aspects of Masonry that we cannot gather from studying the degrees. This is sparked by curiosity that came from secrecy. In the midst of all this, the candidate is said to be amused by the variety of the scene, the pomp of the decorations, the appliances of machinery. Respect was inspired by the gravity and dignity of the actors and the majesty of the ceremony. It's a beautiful spectacle, and this is also a test in itself, appreciating what the ceremony can have in store for us.

As Albert Pike claims, "The very word 'mystery,' according to Demetrius Phalereus, was a metaphorical expression that denoted the secret awe which darkness and gloom inspired. The night was almost always the time fixed for their celebration; and they were ordinarily termed nocturnal ceremonies. Initiations into the mysteries of Samothrace took place at night, and did Isis." According to *Morals and Dogma*, "As is a testament to many aspects in life, Initiation is done by the attraction of secrecy, which was enhanced by the difficulty of obtaining admission. Obstacles and suspense redoubled curiosity. Those who aspired to be the initiation of the sun and in the Mysteries to which they commenced by easy tests and arrived by degrees at those who were most cruel (the life of the candidate was often endangered). But it is termed that it has been done in terms of tortures and mystic punishments to which until after he has proven by the most terrible trials that he possesses a virtuous soul, exempt from the sway of every passion, and it was impossible. There were twelve principal tests, and some make the number larger."

By initiation, it was said that those who were fellow citizens only then became brothers. Connected by a closer bond than before, this was done by a religious fraternity, which brought men nearer together because of this connection. This is an important aspect in Masonry to which we must hold true to our hearts and understand that this is what we have going in our close kin. This is said to unite us very strongly, and the weak and the poor could more readily appeal for assistance to the powerful and the wealthy. Again, religious association gave them a closer fellowship. The initiate was regarded as the favorite of the gods. For him alone heaven opened its treasures. Fortunate during life, he could, by virtue and the favor of heaven, promise himself death and eternal felicity. This is the point of being initiated; by the very mysteries we learn to know, we shall better our lives and the lives we care about once we are gone by this divine power of knowledge.

Nevertheless, Initiation was said to get rid of errors and banish misfortune, and after having filled the heart of man with joy during life, it gave him the most blissful hopes at the moment of ecstasy. The benefits that we reap from these august ceremonies is not only present joy, a deliverance and enfranchisement from the old ills, but also the sweet hope that we have in death of passing to a more fortunate state. The happiness promised there was not limited to moral life, which is the point of having such an honor, so it can be carried out for generations to come. There a new life was to commence, during which the initiate was to enjoy bliss without alloy and without limit. Being initiated, there were rewards of social virtues that were attached to the practice. It was not enough to be merely initiated, it was necessary to be faithful to the laws of initiation, which imposed on men duties in regard to their kind.

Sensibility is the most admirable of our senses. What man is truly worthy of the torch of the Mysteries? All initiation is but introductory to the great change of death. Baptism, anointing, embalming, and obsequies by burial or fire are preparatory symbols. These are to descend to the shades of pointing out the mental change that we ought to know about, the renewal of our existence. Death is the true initiation, to which sleep is the introductory or minor mystery. This is because as Masons, we must realize that the body was deemed a prison for the soul, but the latter was not condemned to eternal banishment and imprisonment. The object of the ancient initiations was to ameliorate mankind and to perfect the intellectual part of man, the nature of the human soul, its origin, its destination, its relations to the body and to universal nature, and all formed part of the mystic science. This was to put them in part by the lessons given to the initiate as direction. It was believed that initiation tended to his perfection, and to preventing the diving part within him, overloaded with matter gross and early.

Initiation was material, but not brute, inert, inactive, lifeless, motionless, formless, or light-less, but rather, it was set to be active, reasoning, thinking; its natural home in the highest regions of the Universe, whence it descended to illuminate, give form and movement to vivify, animate, and carry with itself the baser matter and whether they should be free from itself as to the connection it bears with that matter. That was the doctrine of Pythagoras, who learned from the Egyptian Mysteries, and it was the doctrine of all whom, by means of the ceremonies of initiation, purified the soul. Most importantly, lustrations viewed by what were symbols of those intellectual oldies by which the soul was purged of its vice-spots and stained, and freed of the encumbrance of its earthy prison, so that it might rise unimpeded to the source from which it came. Religious ceremonies and initiations, through the will of God, taught that we expiate here below the crimes committed in a prior life. Again, purity of the soul is the key aspect. This brings us naturally to the tragic portion of these religious scenes and to the allegorical history of the different adventures of the different renders of the principle, light, victor, and vanquished by turns. Here, the most mysterious part of initiations: the veil of mystery and silence.

Thus, the whole system of the Universe was displayed in all its parts to the eyes of the initiate, and the symbolic cave that represented it was adorned and clothed with all the attributes of that universe. To whose world, one is said to exhibit the necessary qualifications and characteristics that purely represent the ideals of Masonry. Teaching this, the Mysteries strove to recall man to his divine origin and point out to him the means of returning to where the soul began. The point of all this is the idea that the human mind will always look spectacularly upon the great mysteries of nature and anticipate the profoundest notion of the mysteries, keeping one's secrets. The point is the philosophical notions of secrecy, the struggle of comprehending life after death; this is done through initiations, to see past the great phenomenons of life, birth, death, and decomposition but mainly to bring one nearer to the Deity and crowning the candidate a common brother.

23

25th Degree
Knight of the Brazen Serpent or Sufi Master

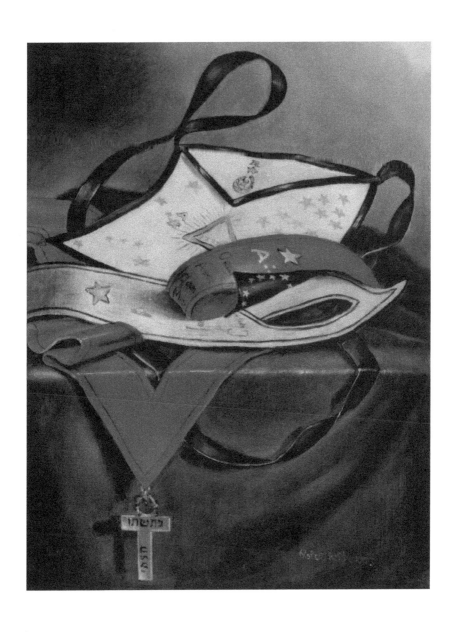

The 25th degree – Knight of the Brazen Serpent, in its most simplest ideals, sets out to teach us to fulfill our destiny and re-create ourselves, as Masons, by reformation, repentance, and enlarging our knowledge. We are meant to learn that a man is merely composed of the flesh, the soul, and its intellect. Further, a man is a reflection of the divine; this was never to be weary of God with petitions. With this in mind, the purpose of this learning of this lecture is derived from its philosophical and moral lessons. We are to learn the necessity of reformation as well as repentance as a means of obtaining mercy and forgiveness (devoted to explaining the symbols of Masonry). For this reason, we are told that in this degree, an enlightened man has no need of ordinary light. By this, Masonry teaches us that the only enlightenment one needs is that of the truth and how its origins come from within, God, and lessons in life, and Masonry being that the light of other men is not what we should consider obtained knowledge. What is to follow is my explanation.

First and foremost, we learn that the soul and the heavens are closely linked to the minds of the ancients because they believed the soul originated from the heavens. As well, the initiates are taught that the mysteries that rule evil and darkness are only temporary, but the light and good will always be eternal. In a nutshell, this is the purpose of knowing what one's eternal knowledge contains, for it's the most vital part. The purpose of all this, especially the rituals, was to purify the soul and impart to man's hope for a future life because the heavens were looked upon with awe by the ancients. But this also has a lot to do with human nature, which we should look upon with the confounding symbols with charity, studying their knowledge in order to formulate our own convictions about the soul, the Deity, and truth. This is the ideal that lies in the notion of externalizing one's knowledge, that being enlightened, not ordinary light from others. On the contrary, the acts of gaining 'ordinary' light or knowledge from outside sources is best symbolized in *A Bridge to Light* as a notion removed from the hearts of the populace and causing the most unimaginable terrors: "That such knowledge became corrupted and occasionally even became an instrument of political and religious repression only serves to demonstrate how little man has changed over the centuries, first gaining a pure knowledge and then corrupted its use for base ends."

As Albert Pike remarks in *Morals and Dogma*, we learned in the 24th degree that the ancient philosophers regarded the soul of a man as having its origins in Heaven. This was the mystery taught to the great doctrine of the divine nature. It longs after immortality of the soul, nobility of its origins, the grandeur of its destiny, its superiority over the animals who have no aspirations heavenward. By this, Pike means that it should be in our most primitive and natural state to follow the Mysteries for our eternal belief and teachings, not those things we get from ordinary light. This would do us no good, as it would fault those who are not worthy of having such grand knowledge. For that, we are to be thankful unto God, for it is He who gives us the proper knowledge, and whoever is thankful for this shall be thankful to the advantage of his own soul. This very complex notion lies with the forces that lie in belief in itself, for we know the force itself by the manifested energies of the force; the soul by its thoughts, matter by its qualities, the cause by the phenomena, the first cause by universal nature. We must know as Masons that we have the right in each case to give the word knowledge a sense wide enough to include the information so acquired. In this, the idea of attraction of forces is what's at play, for we must act on the tendencies of obtaining knowledge, and the mobility of external causes must be derived by God. This is the point of following an enlightened route instead of the ordinary. It is said that he who shall answer dwelling questions concerning knowledge may venture to inquire what the First Cause of all things, the unity of will, the limitless, the infinitely mighty, the infinitely wise designer, in his nature and essence, is. Until then, we are to be content to know him by his revelation in the universe and in one's own soul.

Now, one may ask, how does a person know which is the proper route to take when it comes to belief in a certain knowledge? The answer, though very comprehensive, lies, again, in one's internal belief in God. This is accomplished by the five senses, which the Light also represents. God enables the soul to acquire knowledge, but if it were imprisoned in a body that had neither the sense of sight, nor that of hearing, in a body without the sense of feeling, tasting, or smelling, it would still be an intelligence, and he could impress upon its convictions that constitutes the highest and most certain knowledge. The little ray of intellect would still be connected with one's true source—God and his divine power through knowledge. It is said that the souls of the chosen ones are like mirrors that reflect in minute rays somewhat of the Driving Intelligences; and thus, God has spoken to men by the mouths of his prophets. This is what is meant when considering which lighted path to take; it should be that of enlightenment derived from God, for this is the only way to diverge from dependency on other man's ordinary rites.

We must listen to those who say that matter is self-existent and has inherent forces, by means whereof the senses have their being, as one listens to the rambling of children or of old men in their dotage. Because these cannot comprehend the self-existence of the Supreme Self Existent Intellect, who is at least a possible cause of things and phenomena, they accept the more incomprehensible notion of self-existent matter with impossible potencies. No combination of material atoms could produce the senses, and even less the intellect; and least of all a moral law devoted to God. Even more so, we must know that God chose messengers from among the angels and from among men. God is the light of the Heaven and Earth, and unto whoever God has not shared his light; he shall enjoy no light at all. We must believe in the knowing of what is meant by His light, for it is not fit for man. God should speak unto him otherwise than by private revelation, or from behind a veil, or by his sending a messenger to reveal, by his permission, that which lies for he is all that is high and wise. But gaining such knowledge comes with the triumphs over evil; we must hold true our belief in all that is God. For God is eternal, uncreated, and infinite. His essence is not definable, and he is himself beyond the reach of the imagination. The most profound reflection and mediation cannot comprehend him. We know that the human reason is utterly powerless to form any conception of what he is. It has personified his attributes, his intelligence, will, wisdom, word, might, and sovereignty as if they were created beings, his ministering spirits.

In closing, there is and always shall be a profound and unfathomable mystery in the revelation of the intellect of God, but there is a mystery as fathomable in the revelations of his power. We no more know how we see and hear than how we think. We no more know how our will moves our hand, eyelid, or even body than we know how it controls or is controlled by the wills of others. Light comes to us directly from the sun, but we do not know what light is. We do not comprehend how God reveals himself in the human intellect. That no more makes the human being god than the sun is made to be God because it manifests the light of God. We must apply these words when we go beyond the domain of the senses or be silent for want of words. Intellect emanates and flows from God. Light is an effect, of which he or an emanation of him is the cause. But the worlds of matter, surely not self-existent, have not emanated from him. Therefore, they have been created and are animated by him. Furthermore, in attempting to follow the righteous path, we must know that the believer (which should be us, as Masons) sees by the light of God, and he, by his light, should always be with us. This comes into play with personal triumph with beliefs. We must always have faith and continue in the path we know to be right. This is the very duty of every Mason; we must follow the good path and diverge from that of evil and darkness, for we will never know the negative effects of following ordinary knowledge, yet we know true that the path of enlightenment is of that which follows God. This is vital not only in this notion of knowledge, but also the persona in a duty-filled Mason.

24

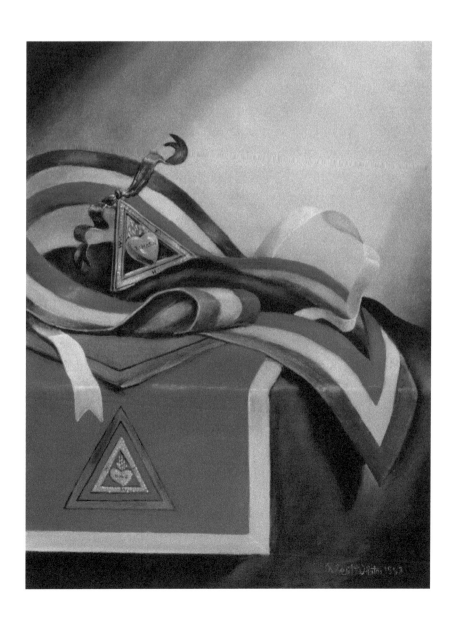

The 26th degree acts on vital aspects of Masonry, that being, the need for toleration in our practice. The idea of this notion is to allow each individual person to interpret the symbols and teachings of the degree for himself. Yet it is important for us to know, as Masons, to learn the concept of the Trinity explored in ritual. Through the three columns of the lodge, wisdom, strength, and beauty, which symbolize the very foundation and tributes of God? These are also seen as faith, hope, and charity, which are the virtues of man and especially so of Masons. We aim to keep this in mind, in that, I mean that this is the very grounds of our beliefs; we must use these virtues in an attempt to keep our faith on an even keel with God. Within these virtues lie, what Albert Pike calls the Masonic Creed, a concept of trinity which is derived from the Nicene Creed of Christianity. This degree focuses on religion and keeping true to that faith by continuously holding true and faithful to our faith and our God.

Within this lecture, we learn that through the teachings of the 23rd through the 26th degrees, we have been introduced to the illustrations and base-line of the nine Great Truths of Masonry. These act on vital aspects that Masonry should always pertain. What is to follow is what should be expected when using this doctrine as a foundation to our guidance, as well as the contextual meaning as it applies to man. The first great truth states: "No man has seen God at any time; that is, God is only spiritual." By this, Masonry sets out to teach us that no man has ever seen God, rather, he is One, all eternal, all powerful, all wise, all just, and merciful. This tells us that we must keep to our beliefs, as God is our source of light, the one that created the universe and all living things as well as the souls of men—this is something that is permanent and unchangeable, so the rest is up to us to keep our faith and hold true this great truth.

The second great truth states that "the soul of man is immortal." This notion acts on the very nature of man and our origins. We are human, but our soul is immortal; by this, Masonry sets out to state that this isn't a phenomenon; we were created by God, and this is something that is an actual existence. It's as if we were living spirits, a spark of central light, and that our bodies are the dwells of what we do. This separates us from death, to which eventually it will be returned by the God who gave it. This was very confusing at first, but after I started to think about it, the more I realized that it's as if we are vessels, and because of this we must stick true to our creator, and yet we possess activity and intelligence; we would not have a body to put it all in. This is something that God did, and because of this, we hold a responsibility to do his duties, for we are granted with the blessing of this body and soul. This leads into the third great truth, which implies the impulse that directs us to conduct ourselves correctly is not only older than the ages, but the coeval of the Divine Being who sees both Heaven and Earth. Further, we are warned by this truth of doing crime, wrong-doing, and violence, for this is the principle that impels us to feel guilty when we do something of wrong conduct; by this we earn a stamp of virtues, something every Mason must remember.

Following the third truth is the fourth, which states that the moral truths are as absolute as the metaphysical truths. This explains the principles of morality. The moral laws are the necessary relations that flow from the nature of things, and they are not created by people but have existed eternally with God. By this truth, we are told that by doing good, we are in the expression of his will, in so far as that will itself is the expression of eternal, absolute, uncreated justice, which is God. We must carry on his truths, and by this, his justice, for it's a vital aspect of his will, something that contains his intelligence and wisdom. This is the very nature and most intimate essence—that the moral sense is what should drive us, therefore deriving from God, which is a divine source with a divine imperative. Following this is the fifth truth, which explains the distinction between good and evil. This is key: Having the ability to make the distinction is a very unique quality we must hold true, for we can be granted the ability to do good by which can be made meaningful by God's ability. As Masons, we know that there is an absolute obligation to conform to what is good and just, and as we are free beings, the actions of which are up to the man in question. We must know that there is a conscious duty, and because of this duty, we must obey the dictates of truth and justice; therefore, we must necessarily have the power to do so, which involves the power of not doing so. Again, this is the very distinction of differentiating our lives by good and evil, justice and injustice, and the obligation that accompanies it.

The sixth great truth of Masonry states that there are no degrees in the practice of moral obligations; it is neither a variable nor contingent, and no excuse can justify one's failure to exercise the moral imperatives of a just life. This is the very necessity of practicing the moral truths: obligation. This lies in the fact that with principle lays morality. That every act contrary to right and justice deserves to be repressed by force and punished when committed equally in the absence of any law or contract. We must remember, as Masons, that a man naturally recognized the distinction between the merit and demerit of actions as he does that between justice and injustice, honesty and dishonesty, and without such teachings and in the absence of law, we cannot do wrong without being unpunished. So, it is in our own control to follow as the necessary moral laws and know that punishment shall be the result of sin. The seventh great truth states that we should be good, be charitable, and obey the dictates of the generous and noble sentiments of the soul. This means that besides respecting the absolute rights of others and being merely just, we should do well, be affectionate to one another with love, and relieve the necessities of the needy. To be generous, liberal, and hospitable: these truths explain the benefits of kindness and how far something like generosity and morality can go. With this in mind, we must be taught from infancy of the world according to Masonry.

The eighth great truth is the law that controls and regulates the universe of God, motion, and harmony. With this truth, we must remember that evil is merely apparent, and all is, in reality, good and perfect. For pain and sorrow, persecution and hardships are but the means by which we can gain nobility. This is what Pike considers as the way we can build and develop virtues. He goes on to state that without sin, error, and wrong-doing, there can be no effect, and without adequate cause, there can be no patience under distress, no courage to face danger, no truth when speaking, no temperance to avoid excess, and no charity for the needy and destitute. This foundation again aims toward the virtues bestowed upon us by God, to show us how mankind is the riches of the world, and together and with one another, we can better each and every life connected. This is all part of the Masonic obligation: to do unto your brother as you would do to yourself. And by never having a limit or rule, there is no telling how this virtue can carry us; it can help judgment, construction, motives, love, courage, and passion of man, which is something very hard to do with the world we live in today, filled with outside negative influence and soaked in evil.

Last but not least, the ninth great truth: "This is the paradox of the equipoise of the infinite justice and infinite mercy of god; the former alone would call for man's utter destruction, the latter alone would permit the most offensive hedonism. Together they provide man with both retribution and forgiveness." This virtue was the most detailed, as Pike best states ; God is good, and yet there are manmade causes that constantly occur in this world of which we should worry: crime, cruelty, oppression, tyranny, and injustice can often be prosperous in a world such as ours, but happy, fortunate, and self-contented people enjoy all the blessings of God's beneficence, while the virtues and good are unfortunate, miserable, pinning away are perished with the cold, hungry, and as part of slavery. This instrument is the state of oppression to which the victims are the miscreants that govern it. We must remember to go beyond and strive past doing something wrong and filled with injustice because a world without such merit from God would only perish in the sands of time. We must remember that there is another life that is filled with wrongs and must be repaired; this is the power of man's will, and we must use our virtues to tend to infinity, an instinct of immortality, and the universal hope of another life. This is something that is testified by all creeds, traditions, and poetry. This is something that no orphan should go without: a father. And this is something that must happen in order to see when light and truth and the just and good shall be victorious, and darkness, error, and wrong will be known no more.

Ultimately, life is one great harmony, and we must use what God has blessed us with to accord to all the faiths of all nations, deep-rooted in the hearts of our most primitive ages. WE MUST remember that light will ultimately prevail over darkness and the good principle over evil—and by doing so, we will again return to a perfect bliss in the bosom of God, to offend against whose laws will then be no longer possible.

25

27th Degree
Knight of the Sun (or Prince Adept)

Firstly, the lessons of this degree teach us that God is the author of everything that exists. He is the eternal, the supreme, the living and awful being who created the universe, which is hidden. This incorporates the idea that God is the principle of everything that lives and exists, and being the father of all beings, he is considered eternal, immovable, and self-existent. There are no bounds to his power; in the beginning, man had the WORD, and that WORD was from God. Out of that living power came the light of his existence. We know, as Masons, that we must let no man speak the word, yet it is our job, rather, our duty, to learn and teach others. This is taught by science. We learn that there are seven virtues, four cardinals and three theological, taught in Masonry. Science teaches us such things: That the ancients use the number four to represent the physical world. We have the ability to touch the world, because they believed that everything in the physical world was made up of the same four elements: earth, air, fire, and water. Thus, the number became a symbol by which the physical world was represented.

Further, the spiritual world and God was represented by the number three from the belief that there were three essential attributes in God, something we must remember and act upon. There was the intellect that desired to create and thus the power to create and the actual coming forth of that creation when the will and the power combined. Since four represented the physical world and three the spiritual world, then seven came to represent the whole, everything that was, is, and will be. This is something taught by truth, through God, and learned by the facts of science.

In this philosophy, there is an unavoidable truth and conclusion about the human mind. It is not the opinion of specifics, but rather, people's science and what people know. In virtue of this in-dwelling God in matter, we say that the world is a revelation of Him, its existence a show of His. He is in His work. The manifold action of the Universe is only His mode of operation, and all material things are in communion with Him. All grow and move and live in Him, and by means of Him, and only so. Let Him withdraw from the space occupied by anything, and it ceases to be. We must, as Masons, let Him withdraw any quality of His nature from anything, and it ceases to be. All must partake of Him, He dwelling in each, and yet transcending all. With the objective of science in relation to oneself, there is the failure of fanciful religion to become philosophy. But this does not preclude philosophy from coinciding with true religion. Philosophy, or rather its object, the divine order of the Universe, is the intellectual guide which the religious sentiment needs; while exploring the real relations of the finite, it obtains a constantly improving and self-correcting measure of the perfect law of the Gospel of Love and Liberty and a means of carrying into effect the spiritualism of revealed religion, and in this sense, this is a science. It establishes law by ascertaining its terms; it guides the spirit to see its way to the amelioration of life and the increase of happiness.

While religion was stationary, science could not walk alone; when both are admitted to be progressive, their interests and aims become identified. Aristotle began to show how religion may be founded on an intellectual basis, but the basis he laid was too narrow. Bacon, by giving to philosophy a definite aim and method, gave it at the same time a safer and self-enlarging basis. Our position is that of intellectual beings surrounded by limitations; and the latter being constant, have to intelligence the practical value of laws, in whose investigation and application consists that seemingly endless career of intellectual and moral progress that the sentiment of religion inspires and ennobles. The title of Saint has commonly been claimed for those whose boast it has been to despise philosophy; yet faith will stumble and sentiment mislead unless knowledge be present in amount and quality sufficient to purify the one and to give beneficial direction to the other.

This is what Pike considers as science having matured inferences from experience that all other experience confirms. It is understood to have no fixed system prior to revision, but that mediation between ignorance and wisdom is the aspect that science fills. It teaches us whose immediate object is happiness, and its impulse is the highest kind of love. Science is the realization of life and unites all that was truly valuable in both the old schemes of mediation and the mystical theory of spiritual, contemplative communion. This is something we must believe in, as Masons; we follow the notion that the study of nature and science is a mystery no less important than any other persons. Its main objective is to display the wisdom and power of the GREAT CREATOR. Their lessons and demonstrations were obscure, but GOD is always and will always be clear and unmistakable.

Nevertheless, to science, we owe it to the idea that no man is no longer entitled to consider himself the central point around which the whole universe of life and motion revolves. The immensely important individual is important to GOD and GOD should be to him, and because of this, we must consider our convenience in his Truth. On one side, science has shown us an infinite universe of stars and suns and worlds at incalculable distances from each other, which is also of further mystery, and something we come to learn and appreciate as an unmistakable truth. While, on the other side, the microscope has placed us in communication with new worlds of organized living beings, gifted with senses, nerves, appetites, and instincts, in every tear and in every drop of putrid water fed to us by GOD. Thus, science teaches every Mason, or should, that we are nothing short of an infinite portion of a great whole, something much greater than any individual person. This is something that stretches out on every side and angle of us, and above and below us, there is an infinite amount of complications and which infinite wisdom can always come alone that can comprehend, further being something, we must be true to. There is an infinite amount of wisdom from science that has arranged the infinite succession of beings, involving the necessity of births, decays, and deaths. This made the loftiest virtues possible by providing those conflicts, reverses, trials, and hardships, without which even their names sound never would have been invented without science.

Furthermore, through science comes knowledge. Albert Pike is a firm believer that knowledge is convertible into power and axioms into rules of utility and duty. Modern science is social and communicative. Is moral as well as intellectual, something every Mason must possess. It's something powerful, yet pacific and disinterested. Most importantly, it's something that binds man to man as well as his connection to the universe by filling up the details of obligation and cherishing impulses of virtues. This is also seen when affording clear proof of the consistency and identity of all interests, again, coming from knowledge sparked by science, told through truth by GOD. Through things such as science, we learn that we can substitute co-operation for rivalry, liberality for jealousy, and tending far more powerful than any other means to realize the spirit of religion, by healing disorders. This will be found by the rooted bottom of an ignorant assumption, something that we must hold to our daily lives, educating others. Although, Pike believes that "we shall probably never reach those higher forms containing the true differences of things, involving the full discovery and correct expression of their very self or essence. We shall ever fall short of the most general and most simple nature, the ultimate or most comprehensive law."

The point is that the essential obstruction comes from improvement and discovery; this is something that must accompany all stages of man's onward progress. The most intriguing point made by Pike was the idea that knowledge is always imperfect or complete only in a prospectively boundless career, in which discovery multiplies doubt and doubt leads on to new discovery. The boast of science is not so much its manifested results as its admitted imperfection and capacity of unlimited progress. With this comes morality, and like other sciences, there is a termed moral truth. Moral truths are considered in themselves equally as certain as mathematical truths, but the difference with this comes from the characteristic that as soon as we perceive them, or hear of these truths, they appear to us as vital and something we must set as our rule of conduct, personally. It is a true deposit of what is returned to us, what drives us, and the very eye of reason for our everyday lives, something live and absolute.

> A passage in *A Bridge to Light* states, "if you give serious thought to and reflect upon the teachings of this degree, you will gain insights and knowledge that will change your life."

This degree proves to be a very important one, not only because it encompasses the lengthiest of all degrees, but it's nearly a quarter of Albert Pike's *Morals and Dogma*. Because of this, *A Bridge to Light* suggests many concepts and notions of this degree that have done nothing short than proving itself as a very vital chapter to an overall view of many of the symbols, views, and teachings offered by Masonry. The twenty-seventh degree – Knight of the Sun (or Prince Adept) is very important because it focuses on numerous philosophical questions positioned by Pike. These views are concerned with the Deity, the creation, the existence of good and evil, the nature of man, the soul, free will, moral law, and the hereafter. Above all else, this chapter from *A Bridge to Light* tells us that concepts from this chapter can help us gain knowledge and insights that can change our lives. This was very daunting at first, but then, I proved how easy it was to grasp the notion that this chapter has applications that can help in any contemporary life. With the overall encompassing views of this degree, we learn that every Mason has the ability to become a true adept of the mysteries, to which one can argue and can change our lives through personal experiences. These ideas are as follows.

The first is the concept of religion and the never-ending problem with the human mind. We learn that every religion was a foundation of philosophy, and because of this, their origins may be unknown to a person or even their mind. It's more about feeling or deep emotions. Further, Pike claims that "the history of religion is the history of the human mind; and the conception formed by it of Deity is always in exact relation to its moral and intellectual attainments. The one is the index and measure of the other." By this, I believe Pike means to state that religion, although often a spark of separation between humans and their minds, is also something immeasurable, something that exhibits unalterable dogmas with the notions of philosophy that it encompasses. By this we learn, as Masons, that we must never treat any other human differently because of religion. Having many different religions in this world, although it's often a major contributor to many social dilemmas, should rather be considered as a personal philosophy and something we can still use to come together. As we have learned, there is no bias; we must use the Masonic code to accept and help all others, despite race, color, location, ethnicity, and their belief in religion.

With this in mind, the twenty-seventh degree also sets out to teach us, rather, remind us, of the obvious about the Deity and creation in general. It reminds us that God is the author of everything that lives and exists, that being the eternal, the supreme, the living and awful being. This being something that is hidden in our overwhelming universe, just like our God, there are no idols or visible images, but rather a worship of him that we must do and stay persistent with in the deep solitude of sequestered life. Pike states it best: "He is invisible and fills the universe as its soul, and liveth not in any temple." By this, he means that it's not his job to stay invisible; rather, we must respect and know that he is not visible. We must keep true to our belief in him and hold true the ideals he secretly teaches us through his invisibility and his soul. We have to back up our faith; that is the only way we can be true.

This may, to some, be a way of changing one's lives, but for those who have always had their faith, this is more like a reminder. This is why we consider the Ineffable Name something that is embodied, and it's our job to do the embodying and keeping true to our promise and faith in him, for he will answer and guide us through his soul. Nonetheless, we should remember, as Masons, that he does a lot more for us that we can ever realize. This is something that was taught to me, the concept of his overarching presence, even though we may not see it or even realize it. This degree has taught me that his thought is manifested in his outward actions in the universe, so he is the generative power, spirit, productive matter that drives all that lives in this world because "he was and is all that was, that is, and that shall be: in whom all else lives, moves, and has its being" (Pike). Nevertheless, we learn of truth, something that can always be life-altering. As well, we are reminded that God and Truth are inseparable, that there is a knowledge that we cannot get by ourselves; rather, it's something that comes from God: the saving oracle of truth. In proportion to the thought and purpose of the individual are trained to conformity with the rule of right that is given to us by God, for his happiness is promoted and the purpose of his existence is fulfilled. In this way, a new life arises in him; he is no longer isolated but is a part of the eternal harmonies around him, and we must always place ourselves around him for that reason, and further, let his will direct us by the influence he gives to us, informing and molding it in the path of true happiness. If applied, this is something we cannot obtain by ourselves and is also something that can help drive us toward good rather than evil.

Through his guidance and knowledge, we come to moral truth, which is like every other universal and necessary truth, but cannot remain a mere abstraction. We learn that abstractions are unrealities. This is something we must remember, so as to never fall into any falsified notions of moral truths. There must be a being that not only conceives us, but constitutes it. Moral truth has this characteristic: Tt is not only to the eyes of intelligence that one possesses, or a universal and necessary truth, but rather, an obligatory part of our will. It is a law. We must do all that we can to establish this law of holding a true moral guidance. It is imposed on us despite ourselves—its principles must be without us, and we must hold all this to a state of unity, which is absolute truth. This means to follow the good rather than evil.

This moral truth is also having intelligence. This absolute good must necessarily be an attribute of the absolute being, and by this, Pike means one whom realizes the absolute truth and absolute beauty begin differently from the one who has realized absolute good. Furthermore, this can guide a person to a better life. With this application, we hold true to our promises, our drives, and various aspects in our personal, social, and environmental lives because God is the principle of moral truth and of personal morality. Man is a moral person, that is to say, one endowed with reason and liberty. We are told that man should be capable of virtue, virtue that has two principal forms: respecting others and loving others—performing justice and charity. The creature can possess no real essential attribute that the creator does not possess. This is vital, for it tells us that we must rely on ourselves to drive us in the proper paths of life and never alter our route as long as it's a fulfilling path. This negative effect of such can prove its importance, for this can cause inferiority, short-coming, and imperfections. So, because of this, hold true the word of moral truth, and remember this is a reciprocal system in which we must use our personal drive to hold us on the proper path and never deviate from such, and with this, we can mark our conditions of dependence, thus bearing our moral —something every Mason should be concerned about.

We then learn about morality, and yet again, we are placed in a position of recognizing a duty for morality is a major part of our daily duty. These acts, if done with the best intentions, are all part of our accomplishments. Religion is a prime example of this, for religion is a duty to which we must always hold true. We are told that the spirituality of the soul is the condition and necessary foundation of immortality: the law of merit and demerit and direct demonstration of it. Having these tendencies driving us causes our soul toward the powers of the infinite and the principles of final causes, thus giving us proof of the immorality of the soul, which at that point is considered complete. Furthermore, having duty is our job; not something we must do, but something we should want to do. It should drive us and carry us, for it leads us to embody the moral code and philosophy of Masonry. By this, I conclude that these concepts for the overarching idea communicate that we all possess the ability to perform honorable and Masonic-filled duties, and by this, we can apply such teachings to our everyday lives, thus allowing us to provide the world with one true adept of the mysteries.

In closing, I must add human wisdom, an idea brought to my attention by Albert Pike. He states that human wisdom must always be limited and incorrect, and even right opinion is only something that is between ignorance and knowledge. The normal condition of man is that of progress. Truly being something, we must never lose sight of the ability to grow and move on through the act of progressing. Philosophy is a kind of journey, ever learning, yet never arriving at the ideal perfection of truth. A Mason should assume the modest title of a lower kind of wisdom, for he must forever have something more excellent than he can ever realize he possesses, something still beyond his reach, something ultimately unobtainable that he desires to make eternally his own.

26

28th Degree
Knight Commander of the Temple

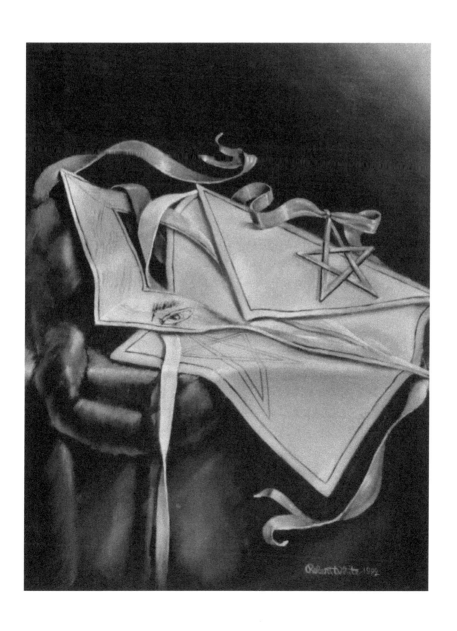

In the midst of the twenty-eighth degree, we learn as Masons that we must always encompass all that we are taught, as the philosophy taught is very applicable in our everyday lives. The twenty-eighth degree is considered the first of the really Chivalric Degrees of the Ancient and Accepted Scottish Rite. Because of this, the twenty-eighth degree is seemingly short in its teachings, both in written papers and published works. It teaches Masonry of the practical teachings of the very core of chivalry and further focuses our attention on ways we should be actively engaging in the duties of life. The notion in this lies within the change in times, and as we know, life is always altering, thus causing its agents to adapt and comprehend. So, because of this, we must come to accept that the times of knighthood and true chivalry are long passed and that virtue, duty, truth, and loyalty are in need in all ages. From *A Bridge to Light*, we learn that even though the times of knighthood has passed, we must incorporate those very virtues as our own, despite which historical time period we are in, because the very foundation of such acts are what develops these teachings into the long-lasting virtues that stand today.

Personally, what drew me into focusing on the changing times of chivalry and changing the very foundation of personal behavior was given to me as a deep thought by Albert Pike in *Morals and Dogma*, for he said that although times and circumstances change, virtues and duties remain the same. It is something that shouldn't change, for we do all we can to better this world despite people's lack or acceptance of such truths. Again, because of this, chivalry is not the same, yet the virtues will always lay the same. And as Pike would proclaim: Evils will remain the same, despite which time period, and even though they may be warred away, they can also take on another shape, thus developing in different forms, which is why chivalry should contain all the same virtues yet should defer from the evils that come with such temptations.

For as long as humans can remember, there has always been a need for chivalry and loyalty; this is a truth that will never consider the historical continuum we live in. As such, we must ask ourselves, what must we do? Because of the significant change in times, we must be able to inherit the teachings from older generations into newer ones. So, the characters of religion and the military, attention to the sick and wounded in the hospital, and the war against infidels in the field are all things that humans will be affected with. But with these trials and tribulations one must overcome in life, the duties within them should be the same. This very duty, taught to us through Masonry, is what is needed in such times of disparity: Hold true to one's chivalric acts, be truthful, and love one another—this is just a gist of the very notion, for we must focus on particular circumstances and perform such historical duties in different forms and shapes in order to exist and environ all. This is the way we must incorporate the very teachings of this degree in the 21st century.

This very idea of chivalry doesn't state or tend to state that there is a need for chivalry, but rather, there is a need to hold true to these virtues as they were in historical times and how they are applicable today. For example, Albert Pike states many instances where the virtues are one in the same. He states that the innocent virgin is no longer at the mercy of brutal men or men at arms, but the point still stands that the purity and innocence of that very virgin still exists, and with this, still needs protectors. Going along with this is the notion to protect one's family. In the 21st century, we may not have battles, wars, or the everyday problems people of the past faced on a day-to-day basis, but we still have those battles, all of which need to have a forefront of men who are ready to face such circumstances. In addition, Pike goes on to state that war is no longer the apparent natural state of society—things are different, thus, our notions of applying virtues must be different. Although some virtues may be an empty obligation to assume, they will have to have the same high duty and obligation that rests in all men. This is something that will not change despite how many years or centuries have passed; chivalry is continuous and never-ending, something we must always hold true to our hearts and encompass our very drive in everyday battles. This is the same then as it is now.

A great vice of this age is the mere absence of truth, profession, and opinion, for they are seen as rarer now than in the days of chivalry. Falsehood is a big part of this, for we have to live with this influence all around us on a daily basis. It has become a current coin of the 21st century. In particular, Pike goes on to teach us about political acts and how men often profess principles that are only profitable for themselves. Not only is this wrong in terms of moral truth, but it shows a lack of chivalry.

Further, at this pulpit, men argue against their own convictions and with what they term "logic," which proves to the satisfaction of others of something they do not even believe themselves. This is truly a vice of chivalry, for it contains insincerity and duplicity is considered to be a norm of their profession. Pike compares this to estates in stocks. It's something that yields revenue and is only beneficial to one person for a short period of time, not considering the long haul. At this point, it is no longer the truth of an opinion or a principle, but the net profit that may be realized from it, which is the measure of its true value. This is a value that contains no chivalry. Nevertheless, our world will always contain acts such as this, people who forget to aim their efforts towards chivalry—and yet again, this is something that should be avoided, for it shows lack of chivalry.

Chivalry, in many cases, can present itself when we least expect it. It is never-ending and all around us. The point still lies in the fact that we must hold true to our Masonic teachings and deter ourselves from persons who incorporate such lack of chivalry. The press is something that will always have this vice. They slander the antagonist and misrepresent what he says and does to invent him into something he is not, to put one in the baseline in an attempt to defeat him—now this is true evil. In our times today, it is our duty, not only as Masons, but as men in this world, as protectors and men of honor. We hold dear that the truth will come from these teachings and from knowing what is chivalric, honorable, and truthful. It is our duty, in the 21st century, to remember all that our ancestors had to overcome and apply those teachings and duties into our current everyday lives.

The most important notion lies in the application of teaching the Degrees and how it will apply to your life. For purity and innocence is everywhere, something every Mason should aim to protect. Not because we are taught this, but because we should want to protect it. It is our Masonic duty to speak the truth, and all the truth, no more or no less, or else not speak at all. That is the code of this degree. Every man in this time can display these virtues, for the opportunity is all around us; it's the mere application of loyalty, chivalry, and truth. So, when a fearful epidemic ravages a city or death takes a loved one or when living becomes scarce, it is the moral duty of men not to flee from the terror but face it and aim to return and live, to become influential and a center of teaching, so that when the danger passes away, we can lay these virtues on those who devoted to stand with me, thus teaching them chivalry, loyalty, honor, and truth.

Ultimately, chivalry is very much alive in our times, although it may be a system of strong derivation, but it is definitely evident and lives strongly with our times and the people in it. It is the very foundation of performing those duties others defer from and to do such things and seeking no other reward other than the approval of our own consciences. Being a true Knight is something that is practiced and encompassed into our everyday lives; to perform the duties and the acts of heroism, as well as devoting oneself to these notions, are what it takes to become a Knight Commander of the Temple. Fight to become a soldier of truth and loyalty, aim to be a protector of purity and innocence, a defier of plague and pestilence, a true nurser of the sick and burier of the dead, and mainly, a Knight, one who prefers death to abandonment of the post of duty. This is what it takes to have chivalry in the 21st century, thus leading to the welcoming of the bosom of this order.

27

29th Degree
Scottish Knight of St. Andrew

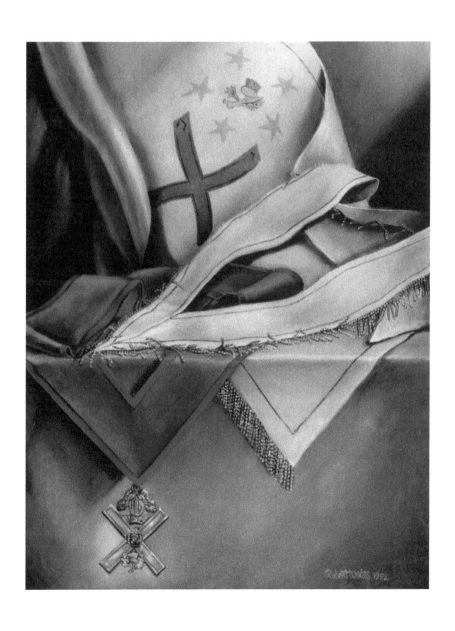

In its most vital historical significance, it must be known that "The Knights of the Temple" or "The Knights of the Temple of Solomon" were originally called the "Poor Fellow-Soldiers of Jesus Christ." Having been established in 1118 once the Grand Master was brutally murdered, the Templars no longer had a common head, nor could they maintain their organization under their old name. This change in name was rendered by King Robert the Bruce when King Edward forbade the organization. The legendary history states that Templars entered into what King Bruce received them into, The Order of Saint Andrew Du Chardon, meaning "of the Thistle" of Scotland. After giving his successors the title of Grand Master of the new Order, this gave the Ancient and Accepted Scottish Rites the final organizational right. This was done by men who were in possession of the Degrees of the Rites of Heredom and Perfection.

In brief, this is the shortened history of this degree. Its significance lies in all the trials and tribulations that these men endured. It is said that "our spiritual life decays in the confinement and darkness of the world," and as these men suffered through the darkness of war, the reign of foreign leaders, and attempts to end a spiritual following, they rose from the ashes of such to become Grand Masters. This idea is the very foundation of this degree: No man can ever rise to their spiritual limit with the overarching influence of darkness in the world. Albert Pike in *Morals and Dogma* speaks very highly of the nature of Saint Andrew. As *Morals and Dogma* teaches, "humility, patience and self-denial are the three essential qualities of a Knight of St. Andrew of Scotland, and holding true to its historical significance, the cross, sanctified by the blood of the holy souls who have died upon it". For example, consider when Jesus of Nazareth, before fainting along the streets of Jerusalem, cried out, "Not my will, O Father! But Thine be done." This statement, taken from Pike's *Morals and Dogma,* shows the unmistakable and rich history of these three virtues by demonstrating that although the physical cry-out occurred, the strength of willpower toward his spiritual belief was untouched by the hands of the brutal soldiers who beat him. Jesus, having consorted with the poor, hungry, and low, is said to have had a life filled with humility, patience, and self-denial.

As the quote above states, and as every Mason should hold true in their hearts, confinement of one's spiritual life is as rich as any other quality of life, even love. This just as every other personal decision we make is on the very persona of Masonry. We must remember our teachings and know that it takes our spiritual willpower to overcome the outside influence of the darkness of the world, as did Jesus of Nazareth, who cried out not because of pain but because he vocalized his triumph over his physical state to say that his spirit will never die; his spiritual standing can never be beaten out of him. This is utter and true Knighthood.

Confinement and darkness are forever all around us. This is something we cannot control, but what we can control is worship and our knighthood. Thus, as Albert Pike states, charity and generosity are even more essential qualities of a true and gentle Knight. Even such acts can be shown by a mark of being noble to those who spare the defeated and conquered. Let it be known that valor is then best tempered when we place fortitude into the hairs of pity; this is what Pike remarks as the ability to shine. Nonetheless, a martial man, one who is compassionate and holds true the morals and virtues of Freemasonry, is one who can conquer both in peace and war and by gaining victory and honor.

To take on the confinement and darkness of the world is no easy task, hence the vital importance of virtue, truth, and honor. It is to our desire and drive to love God above all things, to be steadfast in our faith. This sense of Knighthood is how one overcomes such deterioration of our spiritual realm. Above all else, it was said to the Knights that "ye shall be true unto your Sovereign Lord and true to your word and promise. Also, ye shall sit in no place where that any judgment should be given wrongfully against anybody, to your knowledge." This statement, taken from *Morals and Dogma*, in its most simplest form, answers the question of how to overcome darkness. The answer is something that every Mason must remember: That all it takes is our promise to God, our faith and personal drive to God, to hold true the very foundations of Masonry, which will lead us to him, and as such, fulfill our promise to Him. This promise entails Masonry not to fold onto the evils of life and to overcome the circum-global dares attacking our spiritual standing. There are no qualifications or requirements for such acts; rather, these are simply acts that must be natural to us, for no other reason or derived notion other than personal and moral gain. For this, virtue and wisdom come, but without knowing, only to perfect and defend men.

These garments are a sanctuary that is so sacred that the rich and noble dare not attempt to rob a man of. Our spiritual drive is something that protects and drives us; it is an armor that we cannot lose nor can be broken by sheer pressure or heat. The only way our spiritual divine can be broken or lost is by our own hand, and our own hand only. In such cases, we can never false ourselves to another state other than our spiritual guidance led by God. This is the tenure that holds heaven together. And we, as Masons, cannot claim protection from such heavens without performing such virtuous acts that are proclaimed to us. As Pike states, "Nor is there wisdom without virtue, but only a cunning way of procuring our own undoing." A statement as such demonstrates that only through ourselves can we suppress our spirits, that no force, no act, no evils can ever be presented to us in this world or the next that we can't overcome.

All in all, we should be slow to make inferences from our petty human logic to that of the Almighty (Pike, *Morals and Dogma,* p. 812). By saying this, Pike infers the confinement that can only be halted by our own doing. Despite whatever cruelty we see in this world, and whether or not we have anyone who poke at the ideas of being virtuous, there is no perfectly moral way to follow our spiritual teachings other than our own personal triumph, led and done so by ourselves. Our stature is something that is measured, and every Mason has his own nature, whether it's great or small, but judgment can only be passed by God. There is no way of knowing or even passing judgment of how men are brought into this world and can be immediately known for being great or little in the strength of souls and spirituality. No one can be born into a great soul, nor be born into a lesser one; these are trials and tribulations we place on ourselves to overcome such things as temptation, evil, and darkness. Adding to one's stature should not be the goal, but enlarging one's soul should. This can be done through knowing what is morally right and wrong, leaning away from darkness, and following the light—something done by an act of the will one can endure to make him a moral giant, and thus, dwarf oneself to a pigmy.

Ultimately, this degree sets out to explain that our very lives are meant to set out to follow God, but this doesn't merely mean to simply believe in Him. We must act upon ourselves to do all that is right by God, men, and our fellow neighbor. If there is one thing to take away from this degree, it is that there are two natures in man. There is a higher and lower, the great and the mean, the noble and the ignoble. We are not given which we are; we must use our own voluntary acts of choosing which we want to be and follow accordingly. The choice, rather than the stature of a man, is how he chooses, done so by acts to prove our promise made to God.

As Freemasonry has always explained, we must set forth our efforts to be nobler over the ignoble, spiritual over the material, the divine in man over the human. By following and utterly believing in the chivalric degrees, such as this one, we can use our teachings to help guide us into a status that is, above all, moral and virtuous, a true Knight of Saint Andrew. Magnanimity, mercy, clemency, and a forgiving temper are virtues indispensable to the character of a perfect Knight. The low and evil principle in our nature says, "Do not give, reserve your beneficence for impoverished friends, or at least unobjectionable strangers, do not bestow it on successful enemies, but by friends only in virtue, of our misfortunes." Our spiritual lives, in such a case that it follows the very teachings of Masonry, and more specifically do good to those who hate you and love those who love you, can then not be confined to decay due to the confinement and darkness of the world, for at that time, you can proudly note of the congruence with choosing the higher nature of man, the nature who follows God, done so only by our own doing.

28

30th Degree
Knight Kadosh, or Knight of the White and Black Eagle

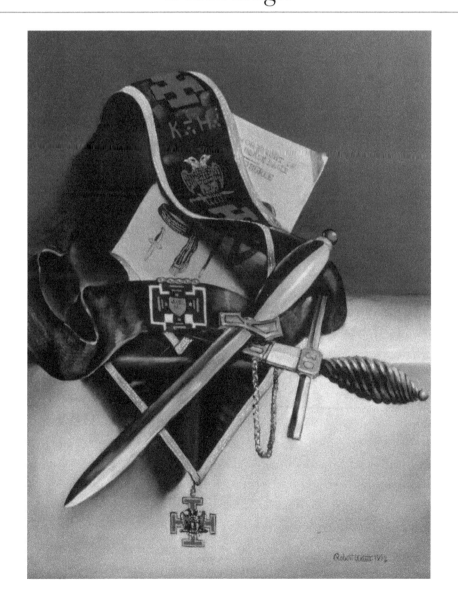

Within the Scottish Rite of Masonry, the thirtieth degree is the last of the chivalric degrees. Its lessons are derived from a very rich history and are said to incorporate the overall teachings of the council. Everything within the teachings of the degree has a greater amount of symbolic meaning to the purpose of the teachings which precedes it. Historically, the figure associated with this degree is Jacques de Molay, the last Grand Master of the Knights Templar, an order created during the Crusades. It was destroyed by Philip IV of France and Pope Clement V in the early 14th century. De Molay was put to death, having renounced his confession that had been extracted under torture. Before his death, he accurately predicted the deaths of Both Philip and Clement within a year.

The word "kadosh" is Hebrew, and Pike says that it is defined as being holy; hence, the Knight Kadosh means Holy Knight, or Knight of the Temple. It is believed that the good and true Knight Kadosh is armed outwardly with steel but inwardly with faith in god, love toward his fellow man, and knowledge. The purpose of the degree is primarily aimed to set the real and noblest sentiments of man. The Knight Kadosh is one who is driven to restore to man all his powers and the whole dignity of manhood and to make true again the ancient description of man that he was made in the image of the Deity. Within the ceremony of this degree, we are told that the symbols of the degree are three skulls, three funeral urns, the mystic ladder, and the double-headed eagle.

In preparation for these arduous duties, a candidate is taken through four apartments. The first apartment has black hangings and a tomb with three skulls. This aims to remind the candidate of what he was taught as he became a Perfect Master, the uncertainty of life and the inevitability of death. The candidate is told that the reward for those who overcome the dread of death is to "ascend above the terrestrial sphere" (*A Bridge to Light*). Furthermore, the center skull is supposed to be that of de Molay and is wreathed in laurel and amaranths, signifying immortality. The skull is dressed with a regal crown that represents Philip and stands for tyrannical kings. The third skull is that of Pope Clement and represents unholy, ambitious religious leaders. As a group, the skulls portray the history of the human race, that constant tragedy of guilty power and murdered innocence. Taking on the role of Knight Kadosh is no joking manner; the candidate upon passing the first apartment is advised that "Thou holdest thy fate in thine own hands," simply stating that every person holds their own fate in their hands.

The second apartment sets out to teach the candidate to learn to pursue with feet that never tire and eyes that never sleep. With hangings of white, this chamber announces the duties of a philosopher and a Knight Kadosh. This sets out the personifications of the three assassins of Hiram, the Incarnations of Evil, which these three were but the tools and so labor unceasingly for the Good of Mankind. This teaching is vital, for its goals are to teach that Masonry does not aim for utopia but rather that people will have such institutions and governments as it is fitted for them to have.

Nonetheless, it is important to know that upon the third apartment, the double-headed eagle symbolizes the times of past and future, for this apartment is where the candidate sacrifices his own personal ambitions and desires on the altar of truth. This apartment has hangings that are light blue and hung with crimson, except in the east, which is hung with black and embellished with skulls pierced by daggers. This is where the candidate is considered a man, for it is said that "He is free from the notions of childhood" (1 Corinthians 13:11). This entails that he is capable of distinguishing the truth and manly enough to follow it, allowing the flow of his empire to be over himself. Seemingly, the most elaborate symbol in this degree is the Mystic Ladder, which on one side represents the seven liberal arts and sciences of the ancients: grammar, rhetoric, logic, arithmetic, geometry, music, and astronomy, all of which were distinguished to Masonry through the third through twenty-ninth degrees, hence the overarching notion that this degree is a summary of the overall teachings of the Council. The following are general ideas that have a vital importance in the teachings of past degrees. Many of these should be easily recognizable.

The first is grammar, which is a function of language to communicate with one another. Communication requires the idea of prediction, which demands rules. We must express our moral values and our understanding of the universe through human communication, for this is the mode and the very foundation in which all expressions come from, something vital to a true and great Mason. Rhetoric, which a man should seek out to use to persuade those in eloquence and the social world to obtain power over others. This is the domain of rhetoric, and without it, neither moral nor political leaders would be possible. This leads into the third: logic. Logic is the point of the first two, to plead his arguments and to have a force behind all reason. Logic is, then, an indispensable tool of moral and intellectual leadership. The next is arithmetic, which is the same of every school and the engine of business. Called the mother of civilization, for the recurrent themes in numbers in daily life regulate mystical significance.

Geometry is next and is considered to be the first and noblest of the sciences (*A Bridge to Light*). This form of measurement is considered for its practical use and became sacred to the figures of the ancients. This derived, Pythagoras who preceded Socrates and laid the foundations of modern Western mathematics, philosophy, music, and religion. Music is the sixth, which is a form of harmonics and derives pure aesthetic and appreciation of harmony in the universe. Jubal was said to create the music of the spheres, which can be a sort of music of God. Lastly, astronomy is considered to be the vault of heaven and a form of great wonder and beauty. With an appreciation and acceptance of astronomy, one is told to stop and gaze upon it with a profusion of tiny lights that sparkle and is man's tracing board. This involves mythology that discerns fate and pure wonder.

Finally, we come to the overarching themes of this degree. Although there are many ways to understand the stance of the thirtieth degree other than its teachings, there is a remarkable truth behind the following notions, all of which are derived from past degrees. The first and most vital foundation of the instructions of the Council is that knowledge is power. Education is said to expand one's intellect and leads man toward the real understanding of what truth is. It is the ignorant man who is the slave of his emotions, which is why it is vital in Masonry not to be ignorant, and further, not to follow the cleverest orator and believe in the most corrupted logic. This is where the idea of tyranny comes into play, for with the presence of ignorance comes the presence of tyranny. Thus, true freedom is the acquisition of knowledge applied to the practical understanding and implementation of life. Next, there is a spiritual war against tyranny, for this in intolerance. This creates broken promises, which, when they do fail, are threatened, and when the threats fail, it excommunicates and attempts to make its enemies anathema to their surroundings. This war against the spirits aims to conquer the hearts of men and sets out to serve its ends and cooperate in the preservation of the institution rather than the preservation of its teachings that may themselves sublimate.

The next idea has to do with forms of government, which entails a war against it. Despots seek to control men's actions. This idea states that propaganda replaces education and freedom of the press becomes a conspiracy against a well-ordered society. War becomes a tool of distraction, facing the nation outward so that it may not see the corruption within. This can be seen with today's society, that great sacrifices are demanded in the name of patriotism but the end is only the sacrifices and the distractions they created. Furthermore, we learn as Masons that we must rage war against vice. This means to struggle, which vice aims toward man's moral nature. The enemy in this case is greed, something every true Mason should avoid, for its weapons are ambition, fanaticism, and superstition. This is a war that man may never win, for the conflict between good and evil may not be fought on this earth as long as ignorance, weakness, and hunger exist and are exploited. The work of the Knight Kadosh is laid out before him, to make the world a better place than he found it. Reason and knowledge must be our guides; the only true victory is a moral one.

We must endeavor to learn from our enemies' flaws. Beginning with the anti-Masonic movement of this time, Pike illustrates steadfastness by the example of Masonry's renewal in the face of prosecution. Masonry benefits by these attacks as weak and vacillating members, but it is the sincere and dedicated brethren who remained who are brought about to rebuild Masonry in today's society. With this, we must set ourselves against having personal vendettas. It is self-destructive in his most natural state. Masonry does not seek to avenge the wrongs of history by warring against the political and religious institutions that spawned them; ratherm, we war against the vices. Lastly, we must remain true in the belief that a man is supreme over institutions. This theme is the truth expressed by the Knight Kadosh, and it claims that individuals are above the idea of being institutionalized. This truth is based on a system of checks and balances, which protects the individual from the tendency of despotism inherent in all political systems. By its separation from religious ties, man's political life is freed from the promise and the threat of spiritual rewards and punishments.

Ultimately, the accomplishments of this degree are seen in the labors of Masonry. The instructions should be received as virtues to which we must all hold true. The reward of such is to approach the holy empire, which signifies the attainment of science and power of the Magi. The four words of the Magi are, to know, to dare, to will, and to be silent, and they are written in even more symbolic forms. With these accomplished, these teachings are what brings us to this point, and the point is that we are brought to the completion of the third Temple, to which the Royal Secret is solved, as to whether we have made this world a Temple fit for the abiding-place of the Grand Architect of the universe.

> "To laugh often and much; to win the respect of intelligent people and the affection of children; to earn the appreciation of honest critics and endure the betrayal of false friends; to appreciate beauty, and to find the best in others; to leave the world a bit better, whether by a healthy child, a garden patch, or a redeemed social condition; to know even one life has breathed easier because you have lived. This is to have succeeded."
>
> —Ralph Waldo Emerson

29

31st Degree
Inspector Inquisitor or Initiate of the Egyptian Mysteries

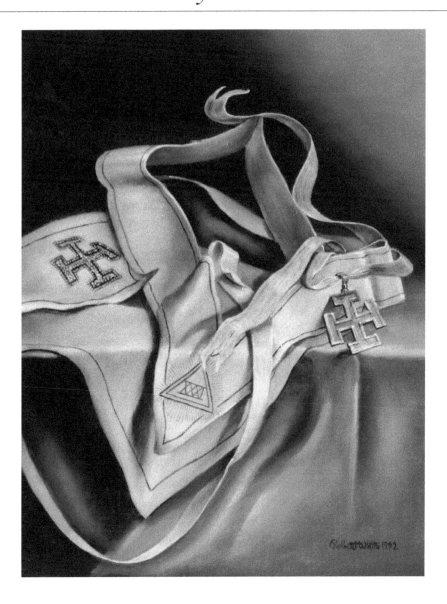

With the teachings of the thirty-first degree – Inspector Inquisitor, we ought to see the introduction to the Consistory Degrees. These incorporate the thirty-first and thirty-second degrees, which are seemingly very different in form and content than the ones preceding it. The idea that lies within the thirty-first degree reveals the dynamic relationship that we must face on a daily basis. This never-ending dilemma encompasses the contrast between human law as a means of achieving justice and divine justice as an ideal. The main objective of the teachings of this degree is to teach us, as Masons, to judge ourselves in the light of knowledge and the lessons of the preceding degrees. Furthermore, it teaches us that the path to immortality is more than a mere out-bound appearance of piety.

With this in mind, the ancient Egyptian belief reflects on the specified relationship between human law and divine law with the claim that a reflection of one's soul's descent occurs with the body at death, at which point his virtues and vices might be weighed to determine if he has any dwellings with the gods. This degree as a whole teaches us that everywhere in the world there is a natural law, meaning there is a constant mode of action. We must remember, Brother, that this fact is universal. We, as human beings can call upon modes of actions, those being the law of matter, the law of mind, and the laws of morals. This tells us that there are different modes of actions that derive from the material, mental, and/or moral forces to which we originate our acts as humans. The ideal laws of matter we know only from the fact that they are always obeyed. To us, the actual obedience is the only way we can know that they are held true; this gives us the only evidence of the ideal rule. Through the laws of matter, we learn only by observation and experience. This tells us that if a body would fall, it would fall sixteen feet the first second, twice that the next, four times the third, and sixteen times the fourth. No mode of action in our human capable minds would this action not be anticipated, for it is the rule of action of the world. The same is true for the laws of matter. And thus, the ideal law is known because it is a fact. The law is imperative, for it must obey without hesitation. With this notion lies the ideal that laws are made to be obeyed. This statement is at its minimal perspective.

This degree aims to teach us that in the spiritual world, which entails the world of human consciousness, there is also a law. An ideal mode of action for the spiritual forces of man lie. The law of justice is as universal as the laws of matter and attraction. Nonetheless, this sets the tone for human understanding and the human condition, for in the most simplest terms, we shall not understand. There is no doubt that the laws of humanity exist, but with the great phenomena of understanding lies the difficulty of the great law of justice. In that, we must know that we do not and will never understand the law. It is very easy for some dreaming and visionary theories to say that it is most evidently unjust trouble in which we know no other way. This is to say that our little measure of justice is not God's measure. His justice does not require us to relieve the hard-working millions of all labors or to emancipate the serf or slave. It would be safe to say that the entire truth of justice is the constitution or fundamental law of the moral Universe, that being, a rule of conduct for a man (As it should be for every living creature). There is no doubt that in this society, there is a law that all human affairs are and must be subject to as the law paramounts, this counting and coping with what stands and the wrongs within acts as they either stand or fall. This is the act of the human condition, for we may not know what we are sparked upon, but it is not within our power to judge the power, but simply obey the laws with the dire-most upbringings.

The ideals of the degree are as such, and for such an explanation, I call upon *Morals and Dogma* by Albert Pike, who, in his teachings, tells Masonry as a whole that it is part of the human condition to find out what the universal law of justice may entail but to undertake the measure of something to our own understanding or level is another. These two things are what we can call the human condition, for it is human nature to be observant and curious. But it is not within our power to pass our own laws and judgment on the divine. Now, I said divine, for God's plan entails the great general plan and system of the great laws enacted by God, something that is continually producing our limited notions of what is wrong and injustice. This is not something for us to control but for us to maintain and hold, for we cannot compare to God's power and his unruly laws. Contradictions are also a huge part of this notion, for we must hold true that God is relentless, and we must trust upon him to guide us to the light. This is to say that in our ideas of justice, there are unjust moments where we may call upon questioning. This human condition is something that is ever-evident. For example, when a child is made miserable for life by deformity or organic diseases, it is not our moral or duty to question how and why this happens, for it is ancient history that states that this occurred due to the vices of its father, and yet that is part of the universal law. The ancients said that the child was punished for the sins of its father, but for the consideration of justice or injustice, we must remember that this is merely the change of the world.

This same notion lies in the example of a man who steals a loaf of bread for the salvation of his hungry family despite the fact that he is a good man who simply sets out to feed his family. Should that man get punished? This controversy can be one to question, but the point still stands strong that he broke the moral law. Yes, the extent of this situation is one to consider alterations, but a moral law is a moral law, none of which can have any sway or pursuit of difference. That man should know that with the guidance of God, he will be given the opportunity to find a path that is more righteous. This, in the sum of the human condition, is what lies with the contradictions that lie with self-improvement confined by moral actions and piety.

Nevertheless, "impracticable rules in morals are always injurious, for as all men fall short of compliance with them, they turn real virtues into imaginary offenses against a forged law" (Pike). This idea states that justice should be in accordance to the God-created relations that exist between them, that being man vs. man or man vs. any creature that faces him. We must remember that these laws are not to confine us, but to further guide us away from the sacral of human conditions, for the whole aggregate of circumstances surrounding humans is never-ending, but we must hold true to our belief that they are fit and right and proper to be done. This view is held with the impression to the general as well as the individual interest. The Holy Bible is meant to teach us of our obligation, that as we judge others, so will we be judged ourselves. It is said to be a necessity, although sad, of inferring the motives, intentions, and purposes of man from the uncertain and often unsafe testimony of all that lies in such acts and words. But before every thought, feeling, impulse, and intention of every soul that now is, or ever was on this earth, there is a counterpart, which should be held only by one true realization, that is, the infinite duration of God and his laws. With this said, we must be aware that through the virtues and wisdom taught to us by Masonry, we already know how to escape from the problems that lie in our future, for these elements that we face are meant to destroy us and our path to what is righteous and moral.

In closing, God has made this great system of the Universe, and with this, he enacted the laws for its governments. Those laws are meant to environ everything that is living in order to network amongst one another in a necessary manner. So, I leave you with this, that what is thus made should be seen in the eyes of every human, especially within Masonry, cannot be unjust, for if these laws are, then God, the great law-maker, is himself unjust.

30

32nd Degree
Master of the Royal Secret

The Scottish rite is intended to teach practical morality and philosophy. Write a paper outlining the ways in which you intend to practice the lessons of the degrees in your daily life.

Freemasonry is the subjugation of the human that is in man by the Divine, the conquest of the appetites and passions by the moral sense and reason, a continual effort, struggle, and warfare of the spiritual against the material and sensual. That victory, when it has been achieved and secured, and the conqueror may rest upon his shield and wear the well-earned laurels, is the true HOLY EMPIRE. This is my moral intuition; to follow my teachings into a level immeasurable by any scale. I wish to take my newfound philosophy to a place where simply using its notions in everyday life, would not be enough; I shall set out to have it carried down for generations to come.

To achieve it, a Mason, as well as myself, must first obtain a solid conviction founded upon reason that he hath within him a spiritual nature, a soul that is not to die when the body is dissolved but is to continue to exist and to advance toward perfection through all the ages of eternity and to see more and more clearly, as it draws nearer unto God, the Light of the Divine Presence. Thus, the Philosophy of the Ancient and Accepted Rite has changed me; and it encourages me to persevere by helping others believe that his free will is entirely consistent with God's omnipotence and omniscience. I must remember that He is not only infinite in power and of infinite wisdom but of infinite mercy and an infinitely tender pity and love for the frail and imperfect creatures that He has made.

You are about to become an Adept of the consistory. We want to stay in touch with you. Moreover, we want your suggestions on how we might improve the college experience for others. Write and send us any thoughts, ideas, critiques, suggestions, and recommendations that you believe will help the college of the consistory grow and prove a viable force in disseminative Masonic education to Scottish Rite Brethren in the future.

Communication is key in any relationship. And although my relationship to Masonry has been a triumphant one, I believe staying in touch will be a difficult task. Staying in touch goes without saying, yet it is the part of both parties to keep in touch. As life gets busier and busier, I believe that we should follow the times of our society and possibly aim toward a more technological approach to communication, which could include blogs, videos, web pages, and informational gatherings. This cannot only help send the word out about prospects, but this can also aid the connection between Masters and newly initiated members. As far as critiques, I cannot add that I have any, but I can say that I am grateful for everything that Masonry has given and taught me, both on a spiritual and physical level. The college of the consistory will grow despite any changes to its methods; a mere effort in reaching out will cause the adverse effect from its alumni.

What is the Royal Secret?

In order to answer the question of what the Royal Secret is, I cannot simply state its answer, for it would have no meaning to the open ear. I begin with the passions of this degree, and they are as follows: A secret in itself is something that is merely hidden from others, something to be kept. This is by no means the purpose in this case. Since the beginning ages of the Scottish Rite of Freemasonry, one of its primary focuses were to help its members to become better human beings and become more morally just with everyday endeavors. We have been learning and teaching these ways without even knowing, and do as they say, "pay it forward." This is considerably one of the major concepts that has nearly gone unsaid. We are told throughout the thirty-second degree that we are every interlaced with the Divine. Now, what exactly can that mean? But this holds a key part in our understanding of the major objective of Freemasonry, and more specifically, the thirty-second degree in the Scottish Rite of Freemasonry.

In this degree, the Master of the Royal Secret, we learn that we must all become members that are connected in more ways than one. This goal of Masonry is aimed to unify its members into one doctrine. Now with these, Freemasonry sets out to teach us duties and lessons, such as our faith and knowledge is one that we should consider as value. Life value. All Freemasons should aim to become a soldier for this cause, and by this, we must become a pursuant of light, freedom, and true religion. At least these should be a goal. This is not a never-ending or never-knowing search but a path set by goals and aspirations that can lead one to a righteous path in life. We must search for our relationship with God; this is morally just. One of the first instructions we received that had to do with the Deity is that the Deity created all and is filled with thought and wisdom, he is all-knowing, and that the universe is created with contraries and opposites, but we also know that he is man's guardian. This view comes from the Hindu and Persian relationship that goes back thousands of years to the B.C.s that entails many different religions. The point of all this is to become blind-folded; we must not judge by what we see, and we must always be open,

open to ones that sound, look, and feel different, ones that believe, love, and treat differently.

The Royal Secret is "EQUILIBRIUM."

According to the Webster's Dictionary, equilibrium is defined as such:
1a : a state of intellectual or emotional balance : Poise <trying to recover his equilibrium> b : a state of adjustment between opposing or divergent influences or elements

2: a state of balance between opposing forces or actions that is either static (as in a body acted on by forces whose resultant is zero) or dynamic (as in a reversible chemical reaction when the rates of reaction in both directions are equal).

Through use of equilibrium, we learn to be harmonious and balanced with everything we do, just as it is in nature. This should be the guide for the right way of living. We must love each other but love ourselves; we must respect one another but respect ourselves. This can be said with nearly every emotion or feeling known. As we wish it upon us, so must we act it upon others. As Albert Pike best states, "of that Equilibrium in the Deity, between the infinite divine WISDOM and the infinite diving Power from which result the stability of the universe, the unchangeableness of the Divine Law, and the Principles of Truth, Justice, and Right, which are part of it, and the Supreme obligation." As he so eloquently put it, these laws are just accepted and taken; these stand with a man whether he chose them or not, and further, these laws and truths are superior to all other laws.

Nonetheless, there is an equilibrium in everything. There is an equilibrium in divine wisdom and divine power because we have been called up as soldiers in which we have to take the role in seeking truth and knowledge. This is done through Masonry. We must also be accepting of freedom and people's demands, for they should be cast as free voices who can key in on whichever aspect in life they wish to hound in on. This must be attained to create an equal and fair keel, and with this keel filled with harmony, we will live life with less evil. Of this, the equilibrium lies in the infinite justice and in infinite mercy, which is given to us by the Deity. This comes from the never-ending use of equity and moral harmony, something given to us by what we should consider the beauty of the universe. This is done through nothing less than a perfect Deity, and by the endurance of the created and the nature of his presence, this is all possible. For Him, it is for us, to love is better than to hate, and forgiveness is wiser than revenge or punishment.

Further, we must learn to be open to all religions, but ever more, the belief in a true religion, for this fights off tyranny with reason and truth. In addition, with this, we learn of that equilibrium between necessity and liberty, between the divine omnipotence and the free will of man. This is something that is relentless and never-ending. We must always seek equilibrium in the true belief of Man, not necessarily one person, but any man. This simply erupts as an example of something that is morally just, allowing people to believe in what they want. To simply put it, it is the free will of man we should strive for. It should be a personal point to say to one's self that nothing can happen without the will of god, for with that in mind, any vices or actions in this world that may be guided by rights and wrongs must first go through Him. There is nothing in the universe that can happen in any other case, and without this co-existence of liberty and necessity, there could be no religion or any justice that is punishable by any penal laws. Next, we must remember that we are to be a soldier of people who encourages man to be self-reliant and independent. This entails the equilibrium between good and evil, the light and the dark. In this world, it should simply remind us of the divine love and divine wisdom bestowed upon us by Him. This should be a reassurance that we must always keep true in our hearts, that in this world, even given this time and age, we must remember that with all the world given to use by Him, there is no amount of evil, body of evil, or even and principle of darkness that can co-exist with the eternal God, or the principle of the light, good and just. This is done by attaining that specific knowledge that we set out to learn. We can, through our faith, see that the existence of evil, sin, suffering, and sorrow in the world that it arrives within, but it can be controlled and demolished through the consistent use of the infinite goodness as well as the infinite knowing of the Almighty, which lives within us.

Lastly, we learn that we must embody a soldier of Freemasonry, and by this, become zealous and ardent in the performance of one's duty to God, family, brethren, and ourselves. In this truth, we should know that the equilibrium lies in the individual action, which is encompassed by free government. By this, we must entertain the foundations of liberty and obedience, law, and equality with subjection to authority and fraternity. This is the aim of the Royal secret, to see the equilibrium in everything, to look at life in the outside perspective, to never see anything one-sided, to be open and wise in our everyday decisions. This is only possible in ourselves, and Masonry forever labors to accomplish in its initiates and demand in its members the equilibrium between the spiritual and divine and the material and human in man. We must satisfy both sides, whether it has to do with intellect, reason, or moral sense, because with this notion, we can live the result of a harmonious and well-controlled life through regulation.

If one were to ask one of his brethren to describe his Masonic journey, he would get a very unique answer to his own. As a matter of fact, if one were to ask a million people, whether they were brothers or not, they would get a million different answers and explanations to their personal masonic journeys. This is because it is what one takes it as, a personal experience. It's the trials and tribulations that one feels throughout life, for it is known that no one is immune to the trials and tribulations of life. In order for one to be considered a prince, or Master of the Royal Secret, he must master the self. This is a right that can be considered an earned right. There are things in life we must include in our everyday lives; these are forces such as power, vigor, strength, and energy. This is a great power, and with it comes great responsibility because once able to pertain to this attribute, it must never be used for evil. By this, I mean that if we are in possession of this power, this force, we must live a moral and ethically correct life. This is only in the eyes, or the acceptance of Him, or the divine notions of life.

Furthermore, if one hopes to become a Master of the Royal Secret, they must possess intuition, reason, and force. Through the uses of intuition and reason, one should be able to figure out and solve the mysteries of the universe to the extent of nature. This law is something that is part of yesterday, a part of today, and will be a part of tomorrow. In nature, we see many things that are easily noticeable. Things that are ascertainable to everyday life, including resurrection, life, death, and the burial of vegetation. This goes without saying, but even nature has equilibrium. So, when we consider the fact that God made man in His own image, man should, through the senses of intuition and reason, arrive with the knowledge given to him through Masonry, and thereafter allow his soul to be resurrected according to Him in order to have lived a righteous life.

For example, one would be a Master of the Royal Secret if he would be willing to protect and serve in the defense of the innocent patron, to feed and clothe the helpless, and above all, suffer a diminishing death rather than defile another man's family, love, or passions. Therefore, the man who is a Master of the Royal Secret will know that precautions to prevent the downhill journey are cheaper and more certain than efforts to apply the brakes after the start is made, or to make repairs for the return trip (so to speak), after the bottom has been reached. He is the one who is constantly on the lookout for those of the universe class and is ever ready to extend a helping hand in the effort to check their downward journey. He is the one who lives up to the teachings of the points of the fellowship and will aid those who are hitting their downhill struggle. This person is one of the few who properly interpreted the words of Jesus when he said, "Thou shalt call no man master but me," knowing that Jesus meant that every person should live a life in conformity with the constructive principles of nature so that they too might say, "I am a master of myself, and I know God's laws, and I am making every effort to obey them," thus having equilibrium.

With this in mind, the man who has lived a moral life and is a master of himself is hailed as a prince, or Master of the Royal Secret, and is bound to excel in all of his undertakings. He will make the bad good and the good better. Should he be in charge of anything, he should instruct his employees and foremen to look after the welfare of those who are working under them, as anyone in power should do. It pays to do good as well as to be good. The better we do, the greater will be our reward, providing we seek spiritual rather than material compensation. This is what it means to be ethically correct in accepting and seeing one's Masonic journey. As best stated by I. Edward Clark, there is a key to heaven as well as hell. The unwise person, one who has not been enlightened, is inclined to the latter, ready for immediate use at all times. To me, it seems that anyone who has this personality and applies it to their everyday life is said to be moral, and by this, I mean that you should never allow yourself to drift into an unwise class, and one should never aim for the key to hell but rather the key to heaven and happiness. So, men who hold the key to Heaven know how to use it in the sense that they are able to obtain the Mastery of the Royal Secret. But this only lies in all who desire it, for it was Confucius who said, "Filial duty is the constant doctrine of heaven and the natural righteousness of Earth, and the practical duty of man." Confucius, like Jesus, was a perfect man and a Master of the Royal Secret.

Many have heard more than one definition of Freemasonry. The truest and the most significant you have yet to hear, for this idea and one's Masonic Journey to the Royal Secret is very case-specific, depending on the trials and tribulations of the member. This is taught to the entered Apprentice, the Fellow-Craft, and the Master, as well as in every degree through which you have advanced to this. It is a definition of what Freemasonry is, of what its purposes and its very essence and spirit are, and it has for every one of us the force and sanctity of a divine law and imposes on every one of us a solemn obligation. It is symbolized and taught, to the Apprentice as well as to you, by the COMPASS and the SQUARE, upon which, as well as upon the book of your religion and the book of the law of the Scottish Freemasonry, you have taken so many obligations. As a Knight, you have been taught it by the Swords, the symbols of HONOR and DUTY, on which you have taken your vows: It was taught you by the BALANCE, the symbol of all equilibrium, and by the CROSS, the symbol of devotedness and self-sacrifice. But all that these teach and contain is taught and contained, for Entered Apprentice, Knight, and Prince alike, by the Compass and the Square.

All in all, every degree of the Ancient and Accepted Scottish Rite, from the first to the thirty-second, has aimed to teach its ceremony as well as by its instruction, that the noblest purpose of life and the highest duty of a man are to strive relentlessly and vigorously to win over the mastery of everything, so that one can become a spiritual and divine over that which is material and sensual; so that in him also, as in the Universe which God governs, harmony and beauty may be the result of a just equilibrium.

The philosophical Degrees have taught you the value of knowledge, the excellence of truth, the superiority of intellectual labor, the dignity and value of your soul, the worth of great and noble thoughts; and thus endeavored to assist you to rise above the level of the animal appetites and passions, the pursuits of greed and the miserable struggles of ambition, and to find pure pleasure and noble prizes and rewards in the acquisition of knowledge, the enlargement of the intellect, and the interpretation of the sacred writing of God upon the great pages of the Book of Nature.

And the Chivalric Degrees have led you on the same path, by showing you the excellence of generosity, clemency, forgiveness of injuries, magnanimity, contempt of danger, and the paramount obligations of Duty and Honor. They have taught you to overcome the fear of death, to devote yourself to the great cause of civil and religious Liberty, to be the Soldier of all that is just, right, and true; in the midst of pestilence to deserve your title of Knight Commander of the Temple, and neither there nor elsewhere to desert your post and flee dastard-like from the foe. In all this, you assert the superiority and right to dominion of that in you which is spiritual and divine. No base fear of danger or death, no sordid ambitions or pitiful greed's or base considerations can tempt a true Scottish Knight to dishonor, and so make his intellect, his reason, his soul, the bond-slave of his appetites, of his passions, of that which is material and animal, selfish, and brutish in his nature.

In closing, this degree teaches many lessons, but the mystery concealed is that man is a creature of free will and capable of recreating himself. If he accomplishes this goal, he will attain a genuine power that can shake the limits of science, surpass the problems of this earth, decipher the secrets of space, surpass the limits of ceremony and catechism, and attain genuine enlightenment; a gnosis, which is the foundation of all religions. He will also surpass the narrow views of interest in the area of morals and will comprehend a genuine virtue that transcends his own interest. Thus, it will become his nature to help his fellow men, and in so doing, he will discover the divine light within which brings true freedom of thought, freedom of conscience, and freedom of culture—to have equilibrium.

31

33rd Degree
Sovereign Grand Inspector General

Description:

The thirty-third degree is conferred by the Supreme Council upon members of the Rite in recognition of outstanding work in the Rite or in Public Life. At its biennial sessions, the Supreme Council elects members of the Rite to receive the Degree. Members unanimously so elected become honorary members of the Supreme Council. The thirty-third degree may not be requested, and if requested, must be refused. The degree is granted solely out of recognition for outstanding services. These 33° Masons are Inspectors General Honorary and honorary members of the Supreme Council. The active members of the Supreme Council are chosen from among them. The cap for an Inspector General Honorary is white with a white band edged in gold, featuring the symbol for this honorary degree, a red slanting Patriarchal Cross.

THIRTY SECOND
DEGREE PLATE

"The Camp": original artwork courtesy of The Craftsman's Apron and
Brother Patrick Craddock.

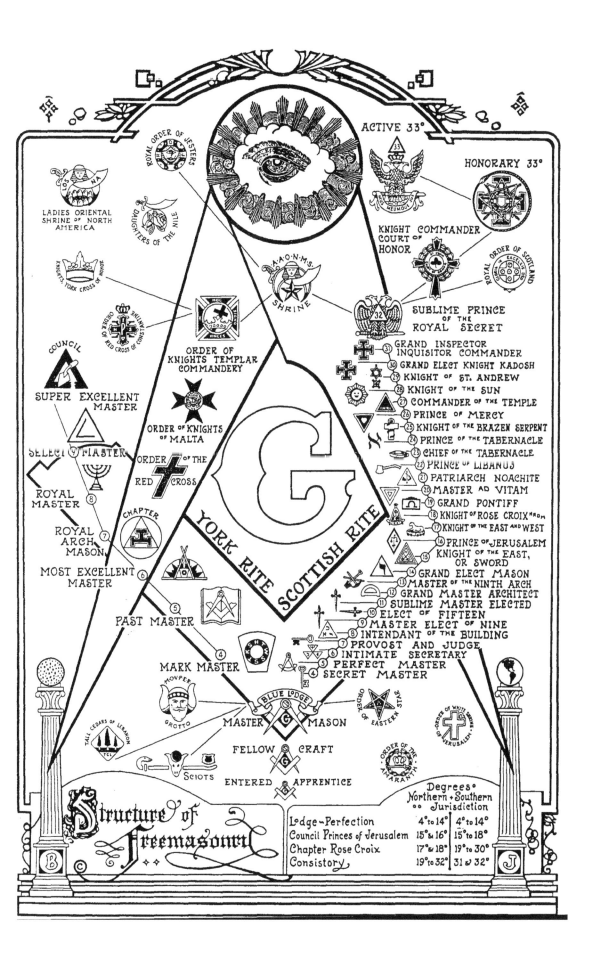

Structure of Freemasonry

Conclusion

I hope you have enjoyed this journey to greater understanding of the Scottish Rite degrees. It is my hope that the philosophy within this book will be a great help to you and provide you the opportunity to become a better person. Indeed, I believe the central themes and teachings of the Degrees governed by the four Bodies which make up the Scottish Rite, from the 4th to the 32nd Degrees, are of great value to us all. If this book has sparked some curiosity in you or inspires you to dig more deeply into the history and beliefs of the organization, then I have succeeded.

Ultimately, though we participate in a large and august fraternity, the journey is a strictly personal one. This road that so few have travelled is unique for each of us. May your journey be one of wisdom and compassion.

Review Inquiry

Hey, it's Brother Sekera here.

I hope you've enjoyed the book and found it enlightening. I have a favor to ask you.

Would you consider giving it a rating on Amazon or wherever you bought the book? Online book stores are more likely to promote a book when they feel good about its content, and reader reviews are a great barometer for a book's quality.

So please go to Amazon.com (or wherever you bought the book), search for my name and the book title, and leave a review. If someone gave you a copy of my book, then leave a review on Amazon, and maybe consider adding a picture of you holding the book. That increases the likelihood your review will be accepted!

Sincerely & Fraternally,
Hon. Michael J. Sekera

About the Author

Michael J. Sekera is a member of the California Freemasons, York Rite, Scottish Rite, Shrine, Royal Order of Scotland, Robert the Bruce, St. Croix Conclave of the Red Cross of Constantine. He also belongs to York Rite College, Sciots, AMD, High Twelve, The Philalethes Society, and others.

He married Abeer Khoury in 1997 in Buffalo, New York. He has three children, Emily, Alexandra and Michael. He considers his children as his greatest life accomplishment, his Monument, and his Legacy. All three are in college as of 2020.

Michael can be reached at: Universityoffreemasonry@gmail.com.

Printed in the USA
CPSIA information can be obtained
at www.ICGtesting.com
LVHW071958131223
766150LV00048B/921